WW Freestyle Cookbook

Produced by Seven Publishing on behalf of WW International, Inc. Published December 2018. All rights reserved. No part of this publication may be reproduced, stored in a retrieval system or transmitted in any form by any means, electronic, mechanical photocopying, recording or otherwise, without the prior written permission of Seven Publishing. First published in Great Britain by Seven Publishing Ltd.

Seven Publishing Ltd, 3-7 Herbal Hill, London EC1R 5EJ
www.seven.co.uk

10 9 8 7 6 5 4 3 2 1

A CIP catalogue record for this book is available from the British Library.

ISBN: 978-1-9996673-2-0

Imprint

WW Publications Team
Samantha Rees, Nicola Hill,
Ruby Bamford

For Seven Publishing Ltd
Food
Food editor: Nadine Brown
Associate food editor: Ella Tarn
Recipe testing: Cate Dixon

Editorial
Editor-in-Chief: Helen Renshaw
Editor: Ward Hellewell
Sub-editor: Sarah Nittinger

Design & photography
Art director: Liz Baird
Photography: Ant Duncan
Food stylists: Emily Kydd,
Lucy Jessop, Nicole Herft
Prop stylist: Tony Hutchinson

Account management
Account manager: Gina Cavaciuti
Group publishing director: Kirsten Price

Production
Senior production manager: Liz Knipe
Colour reproduction by F1 Colour
Printed in the Italy by Rotolito S.p.A

The small print

Eggs We use medium eggs, unless otherwise stated. Pregnant women, the elderly and children should avoid recipes with eggs which are raw or not fully cooked if not produced under the British Lion code of practice.

Fruit and vegetables Recipes use medium-size fruit and veg, unless otherwise stated.

Reduced-fat soft cheese Where a recipe uses reduced-fat soft cheese, we mean a soft cheese with 30% less fat than its full-fat equivalent.

Low-fat spread When a recipe uses a low-fat spread, we mean a spread with a fat content of no more than 39%.

Microwaves If we have used a microwave in any of our recipes, the timings will be for an 850-watt microwave oven.

Prep and cook times These are approximate and meant to be guidelines only. Prep time includes all steps up to and following the main cooking time(s). Stated cook times may vary according to your oven.

Vegetarian Recipes displaying a vegetarian symbol include non-animal-based ingredients, but may also contain processed products that aren't always vegetarian, such as pesto. If you're a vegetarian, you should ensure you use vegetarian varieties and check the ingredients labels. Where we reference vegetarian Italian-style hard cheese in vegetarian recipes, we mean a cheese similar to Parmesan (which is not vegetarian) but which is suitable for vegetarians.

Vegan Recipes displaying a vegan symbol include no products made from or with the aid of animals or animal products.

Gluten free Recipes labelled as gluten free include ingredients that naturally do not contain gluten, but may also contain processed products, such as sauces, stock cubes and spice mixes. If so, you should ensure that those products do not include any gluten-containing ingredients (wheat, barley or rye) – these will be highlighted in the ingredients list on the product label. Manufacturers may also indicate whether there is a chance their product may have been accidentally contaminated with gluten during the manufacturing process. For more information and guidance on gluten-free products, visit www.coeliac.org.uk

Nut free Recipes displaying a nut free symbol include ingredients that do not contain nuts, but may include ingredients produced in facilities that also handle nut products. If you have a nut allergy, check ingredients labels for more information.

Dairy free Recipes displaying a dairy free symbol include ingredients that naturally do not contain dairy, but may include ingredients produced in facilities that also handle dairy products. If you have a dairy allergy, check ingredients labels for more information.

SmartPoints® have been calculated using the values for generic foods, not brands (except where stated). Tracking using branded items may affect the recorded SmartPoints.

When you see these symbols;

4   Tells you the SmartPoints value per serving.

  Indicates a recipe is gluten free.

  Indicates a recipe is vegetarian.

  Indicates a recipe is vegan.

  Indicates a recipe is nut free.

  Indicates a recipe is dairy free.

Contents

Welcome

to the WW Freestyle™ Cookbook. What we eat is very much influenced by the time of year, so we've created a collection of fabulous recipes inspired by the seasons – whether it's a celebration of spring, a summertime social, autumnal Sunday roasts or wintry days with soups and stews, we've got it covered. Eating seasonally means there's always something different to look forward to, and with the wonderful variety of local, seasonal produce on offer, it guarantees your food will be fresh and flavoursome. With 120 delicious recipes, including ideas for breakfasts, side dishes, desserts and snacks, this book will provide you with food inspiration all year round.

Getting started

Here's to you...

Being a member of WW is all about being part of a community, and sharing recipes, tips and personal stories is a vital ingredient in what makes WW work. In fact, some of our best ideas come from you, the members, as well as our amazing Wellness Coaches and the WW kitchen team. With that in mind, we called upon seven fabulous foodies from the WW community to help us create this book...

SELEN OMAR
A mum of two from Reading, teacher Selen has been vegan since the start of 2018 and loves trying out new recipes that are packed with flavour and spices. Instagram: @selly_jelly_go_wwgoldmember

ELISHA LANGRIDGE
WW ambassador Elisha from Fareham is an avid gym-goer, vegan and houmous lover. Her secret to staying happy and healthy? 'It's all about balance.' Instagram: @wwlifestyle92

JONNY SHAND
A Wellness Coach from Greenock, Jonny once described himself as an 'eating machine', but now loves creating delicious chicken stir-fries and rice dishes, using the range of WW marinades Instagram: @_princeofpoints

NADINE BROWN & ELLA TARN
WW Kitchen Team, Nadine and Ella create everything from family meals to healthy bakes. Tasting them is a perk of the job, but what they love most is WW Members talking about how much they enjoy cooking the recipes.

SUE WILKES
Wellness Coach Sue runs Workshops in Leicester. She loves cooking for her family, who can't get enough of her homemade pizzas and turkey mince shepherd's pie. Instagram: @wilkes.sue_weightwatchers

TONY HIRVING
As WW dietitian, Tony keeps a watchful eye on everything food-related to make sure it's healthy, nutritious and well balanced. When he's in the kitchen, he loves to cook anything with fresh fish and loads of veg.

Pancetta, courgette & feta muffins, p30

Honey-roasted figs, p160

All about WW Freestyle™

With WW Freestyle, nothing's off-limits! That means you can still enjoy your favourite foods while staying on track...

All of our recipes are designed with SmartPoints® in mind, so you can enjoy everything in this book while following the WW Freestyle programme. Even if you're new to WW Freestyle, you'll be able to easily cook, track and treat yourself to what's inside.

Still learning about SmartPoints?
When you become a WW member, you're given a Budget, made up of daily and weekly SmartPoints, and you can spend your Budget however you like. You can also roll over up to 4 unused SmartPoints into your Weekly SmartPoints Budget at the end of each day, so you can plan ahead for nights out, special meals or a weekend takeaway – whatever you fancy, you'll have your weekly SmartPoints to fall back on.

ZeroPoint™ foods
While all foods have a SmartPoints value, many have 0 SmartPoints, and these make up the ZeroPoint foods list. They'll not only encourage you to choose the healthiest options, they'll also help you make the most of your Budget.

You can eat ZeroPoint foods until you're comfortably full, and there's no need to weigh or measure them. And because the ZeroPoint foods list includes most fruit and vegetables, many plant-based proteins, skinless chicken and turkey breast, hen eggs, unsmoked fish and seafood, pulses and fat-free plain yogurt, there are plenty of ingredients to use as a base for delicious, healthy meals (see p16 for the full ZeroPoint foods list).

Food you love
We've called it WW Freestyle for a reason – it's the most flexible

programme yet! You can spend your Budget however you choose, whether that's basing your meals around ZeroPoint foods and spending your dailies on snacks, sides and desserts; using your dailies on more indulgent meals throughout the day or spending a few weeklies on a glass of wine with dinner. As long as you stick to your Budget, you can spend it on whatever you fancy.

Help with SmartPoints
To help you get the most from WW, all of the recipes in this book include the SmartPoints value per serving, as well as the SmartPoints for any additional suggested side dishes, added extras or ingredient swaps. Plus, you'll find plenty of help and advice on the SmartPoints values of most supermarket products and restaurant meals online at ww.com or on the WW app.

Turkey & chilli meatballs, p174

ZeroPoint™ foods

These versatile, tasty ingredients are all 0 SmartPoints®. Use them as a base for healthier meals without weighing or measuring.

Dairy & eggs
Hen eggs
Yogurt, fat-free, plain (including Greek and Skyr)
Yogurt, soya, plain

Fish & shellfish
All unsmoked fish and shellfish – fresh, frozen or tinned in water, including but not limited to:

Fresh and prepared
Bream, red or black
Cockles
Cod
Cod roe
Coley
Crab
Crayfish
Dover sole
Eel
Eels, jellied
Grouper
Haddock
Hake
Halibut
Herring
Hoki
John Dory
King prawns
Lemon sole
Lobster
Mackerel
Monkfish
Mullet, grey, red
Mussels
Octopus
Orange roughy

Oysters
Pike
Plaice
Pollock
Prawns
Rainbow trout
Red snapper (Red sea bream)
Rock salmon (Dog fish)
Roll mop herring
Salmon
Sardines
Scallops
Sea bass
Sea bream
Seafood selection
Shark
Shrimps
Skate
Soft herring roe
Sprats
Squid
Swordfish
Tiger prawns
Tilapia
Trout
Tuna
Turbot
Whelks
Whiting
Winkles

Tinned in water, vinegar or brine, drained
Caviar
Clams
Cockles
Crab
Mackerel
Pilchards
Salmon, pink, red

Sardines
Tuna

Poultry
Cooked deli
Chicken breast
Turkey breast

Fresh and prepared
Chicken breast mince
Chicken breast, skinless
Turkey breast mince
Turkey breast, skinless

Fruit & vegetables
All fruit – fresh, frozen or tinned in natural juice or water, drained. Most vegetables – fresh, frozen or tinned without oil or sugar.

Legumes
All legumes – fresh, frozen or tinned without oil or sugar, including but not limited to:
Aduki beans
Beansprouts
Black eyed beans
Borlotti beans
Broad beans
Butter beans
Cannellini beans
Chickpeas

Flageolet beans
French-style fresh beans
Green beans
Haricot beans
Kidney beans
Lentils, green or brown
Lentils, split red
Mung beans
Pinto beans
Runner beans
Soya beans
Tinned beans
Yellow split peas

Meat-free protein substitutes
Plain tofu
Quorn fillet
Quorn mince
Quorn pieces
Smoked tofu

Some fruit and vegetables do contain SmartPoints; these are:
Avocados
Cassava/yucca/plantain/manioc
Mushy peas
Olives
Parsnips
Potatoes
Sweet potatoes
Yams

For the latest sustainable fish guide, visit www.mcsuk.org/goodfishguide/search

Build your meals around ingredients from the ZeroPoint foods list – there's a huge variety to choose from.

A guide to seasonality

Eating fresh produce when it's in season means you'll not only be eating the freshest, tastiest food possible, but you'll also be inspired all year round.

We've all heard that eating fruit and veg at their peak is the best way to save money and source the freshest produce, but as most supermarkets carry our favourite foods year-round, is it really worth it? We think so!

Buying seasonally not only encourages you to try new fruit and veg, it also ensures you're tucking into the tastiest – and often healthiest – foods. As out-of-season produce is usually imported and flown in from other countries, it's often harvested much earlier, meaning by the time it reaches your table, it's lost nutrients and flavour. And while it's true that not all fruit and veg can be grown in the UK, plenty can – and it's all delicious! Choosing home-grown, seasonal foods will help you serve up the freshest fruit and veg and support local farmers, fishers and producers while you do it. It's a win-win!

And, if all of that wasn't enough, seasonal foods are also a key part of our biggest celebrations. Think about it – what would a summer picnic be without strawberries? Or an Easter buffet without asparagus? Or even a big Christmas feast without red cabbage, potatoes and sprouts? Seasonal fruit and veg is at the heart of each and every event throughout the year.

So, if you've turned on to the idea of eating seasonally, check out this list of when fresh vegetables, fruit and herbs are at their best.

SPRING

VEGETABLES
Asparagus
Broccoli
Carrots
Chicory
Cucumbers
Lettuce
New potatoes
Peas
Peppers
Radishes
Rocket
Spinach
Spring greens
Spring onions
Watercress

FRUIT
Kiwi
Rhubarb
Strawberries

HERBS
Basil
Chives
Coriander
Dill
Oregano
Mint
Parsley
Rosemary
Sage
Tarragon

SUMMER

VEGETABLES
Aubergine
Beetroot
Broad beans
Broccoli
Carrots
Courgettes
Cucumbers
Fennel
Lettuce
Peas
Peppers
Radishes
Rocket
Runner beans
Sweetcorn
Tomatoes*

FRUIT
Apricots
Blueberries
Cherries
Gooseberries
Melons
Nectarines
Peaches
Raspberries
Redcurrants
Strawberries

HERBS
Basil
Chives
Coriander
Mint
Parsley
Tarragon

AUTUMN

VEGETABLES
Aubergine
Beetroot
Butternut squash
Cauliflower
Celeriac
Celery
Kale
Leeks
Mushrooms
Parsnips
Potatoes
Pumpkin
Shallots
Swede
Turnips

FRUIT
Apples
Blackberries
Damsons
Figs
Grapes
Pears
Plums

HERBS
Chives
Parsley
Rosemary
Sage
Thyme

WINTER

VEGETABLES
Beetroot
Brussels sprouts
Cabbage, red and white
Carrots
Cauliflower
Celeriac
Chicory
Curly kale
Fennel
Jerusalem artichokes
Leeks
Onions
Parsnips
Potatoes
Shallots
Spinach
Swede
Turnips

FRUIT
Apples
Forced rhubarb
Pears

HERBS
Basil
Parsley
Rosemary
Thyme

*Technically a fruit. We've included tomatoes in vegetables as we dont want you to miss them off your shopping list when planning your weekly meals.

Planning & shopping

Smart meal planning and clever shopping can help you save time, money and stay on track. But where do you start? Here's some helpful advice to make it easier.

Planning

Every day, we make dozens of decisions about what we're going to eat and drink, and every time we do, there's a chance that we might not make the healthiest choices. But planning our meals for the week ahead means we can avoid those spur-of-the-moment pitfalls, making meal times easier, quicker and a lot less stressful. So, what is the best way to go about meal planning?

Write it all down

Start with a blank piece of paper. You may want to plan for the entire week, or just the weeknights – find what works for you. You can use the recipes in this book and your other favourite WW recipes as a starting point. Jot down your evening meals, then fill in lunches and breakfast for the week. Include the Smartpoints for everything, and remember to take account of desserts, snacks and drinks in your SmartPoints Budget.

Manage your time

When planning meals, think about how long things will take to cook, and whether you have enough time to cook each day. Quick and easy dishes are best for weeknights; save slow-cooked dishes and roasts for the weekend. Try to build in variety – you don't want to eat the same thing every day – but also think about whether you could batch cook something and have it twice in the week. Some batch-cooked recipes, such as a Bolognese sauce, could be used to make a variety of dishes.

Make a list

Once you've made your plan, make a shopping list of everything you'll need. Check your storecupboard and freezer to see what you already have – it's a good time to have a clear out of anything that's out of date. Write the shopping list in the order of the aisles at your supermarket to make it quicker and easier when you're shopping. If you only visit the sections of the supermarket you need to, there's less temptation to put unwanted items in the trolley. Or you might want to consider shopping online.

Saving pennies

Buy ingredients you use all the time in bulk – large bags of frozen veg or larger packs of meat can be split into usable portions and kept in the freezer for future meals, while storecupboard staples like pasta and rice can be stored in airtight containers. Shop mindfully to avoid falling for the tricks that supermarkets use to get you to buy things you don't really need, like two-for one deals.

Planning meals will make life a whole lot easier. For some example meal plans, see p208.

Lentil Bolognese, p132

Batch cooking & freezing

You may not always have time to cook a meal from scratch on busy weekdays, but what's the alternative? Set aside a couple of spare hours on a weekend to batch cook and you'll have dinner for the week ahead sorted. If you've been thinking about doing it, now's the time to start! Here's some useful advice...

What sort of things are good for batch cooking?
We've indicated which recipes in this book are good for freezing, but in general, dishes such as casseroles, stews, curries, soups and pasta sauces are all ideal for freezing, while foods containing starchy carbs like rice and pasta, fruit and vegetables with a high water content, eggs and soft cheese do not freeze well.

Planning & shopping
Make a plan – figure out what you're going to cook and what ingredients you'll need. Make a shopping list and shop for everything all at once. Check your storecupboard first to make sure you've got all those staples you'll need, like rice, dried herbs and spices and tinned tomatoes. Clear out your freezer beforehand so you'll have enough room to store your batch-cooked food.

What you'll need
Plastic sealable containers or freezer bags are ideal. If you have microwave safe containers, you can reheat the food in the same container you've frozen it in. Zip-lock freezer bags are great for freezing things in individual portions – consider buying reusable silicone ones that can be washed out and used over and over again.

How to freeze
Let foods come to room temperature before freezing, then put them into containers or bags and freeze them straight away. If you're using freezer bags, squeeze out as much air as you can to help avoid freezer burn and save space in the freezer. Label everything clearly with the recipe name and date of freezing and the portion size. You might want to freeze some single serve portions, or bigger portions for

Your freezer is your friend
Soups, stews and pasta sauces are all great candidates for freezing. Divide into usable portions and label accordingly.

the whole family – freezing in individual portions helps you avoid waste and makes defrosting times shorter. Don't forget what you've got in the freezer. Keep an inventory, or regularly check your freezer to remind yourself what you've got in there.

How long can I freeze food for?
In theory, food can be safely frozen indefinitely, but long-term freezing can affect the flavour and texture of foods and lead to freezer burn. Up to 3 months is good general rule to follow.

'I love that you can have something healthy and hearty on the table during the week, even when you havent had time to cook.' SELEN

Defrosting food
Defrosting food completely before reheating it means that it will reheat more quickly and evenly. It's best to defrost food in the fridge (put it on the bottom shelf) – never leave food out of the fridge to defrost. If you're in a hurry, you can reheat directly from frozen.

Reheating food
When reheating, make sure that food is steaming hot throughout. Soups, stews and casseroles should come to a rolling boil. Microwaves don't heat food evenly, so give the food a good stir a couple of times during reheating to ensure all the food is heated properly.

Spring

Bright mornings, budding flowers, renewed energy – after months of colder weather, spring marks a fresh start. Milder temperatures mean you'll be more tempted to get outside, and with plenty of tasty fruit and veg in season, you'll probably be looking for lighter meals to tuck into that take advantage of all that's available. And, as there are so many celebrations in spring – from Mother's Day to Easter – you'll want impressive (but simple) meals to serve the whole family, like roast lamb, veg-packed risotto and flavourful soup.

'As the temperature rises it's also time to start thinking about salads and seasonal fruits too. My "creative cook" side really starts to kick in.' SUE

Spring breakfasts

Nothing says 'get up and go' like a sunny spring morning. Just make sure you have a good breakfast first! Try these tasty ideas – some you can eat in, others you can take with you...

Something special

'This recipe has an indulgent twist that makes it perfect for special occasions like Mother's Day. My mum was super impressed!" JONNY

Eggs royale

serves 4
prep time 10 minutes
cook time 20 minutes

Put 3 **egg yolks**, 1 tablespoon **lemon juice**, 175g **0% fat natural Greek yogurt** and ½ teaspoon **Dijon mustard** in a bowl. Bring a small pan of water to a simmer. Set the bowl over the pan and whisk until the sauce has thickened. Remove from the heat and cover to keep warm. Bring a deep pan of water to a boil and add 1 tablespoon **white wine vinegar**. Break 1 **egg** into a ramekin. Swirl the water with a spoon to create a whirlpool and slide in the egg. Cook for 2-3 minutes, then using a slotted spoon, transfer to a plate lined with kitchen paper. Repeat with 3 more **eggs**. While the eggs cook, toast 2 halved **wholemeal English muffins**. Spread a little of the sauce over each muffin half and divide 100g **smoked salmon** between them, then top each with a poached egg. Stir 2 tablespoons snipped **fresh chives** through the remaining sauce, then spoon over the eggs. Sprinkle over extra snipped **fresh chives** to serve.

3 SmartPoints value per serving

Pancetta, courgette & feta muffins

makes 12
prep time 15 minutes
cook time 20 minutes

Preheat the oven to 200°C, fan 180°C, gas mark 6. Put 350g grated **courgettes** in a large bowl with 50g grated **Parmesan**, 75g **self-raising flour** and a small handful of chopped **fresh flat-leaf parsley**. Season well, then stir to combine. Make a well in the centre, then add 3 lightly beaten **eggs** and 100g **0% fat natural Greek yogurt** and stir to combine. Fold through 150g crumbled **light feta**. Mist a 12-hole nonstick muffin tin with **calorie controlled cooking spray** and line each hole with 1 slice **pancetta**, then fill with the courgette and egg mixture. Bake for 20 minutes or until golden. Cool slightly, then serve with extra **fresh flat-leaf parsley** leaves scattered over the top. The muffins will keep in an airtight container for 2-3 days.

3 SmartPoints value per muffin

Scrambled egg & spinach wraps

makes 4
prep time 5 minutes
cook time 10 minutes

Mist a large nonstick frying pan with **calorie controlled cooking spray** and put over a medium heat. Crack 8 **eggs** into a small bowl, season to taste, then lightly whisk. Pour the eggs into the pan and allow to set slightly, then stir using a spatula. Add 70g **young leaf spinach** and a small pinch of **ground nutmeg** and cook until the spinach is just wilted and the eggs are set. Divide the egg and spinach between 4 **WW White Wraps**, then sprinkle over 80g grated **half-fat Cheddar cheese** and some **ground black pepper**. Roll up each wrap, folding in at the bottom, then serve.

5 SmartPoints value per wrap

Homemade granola

serves 15
prep time 10 minutes
cook time 25 minutes

Preheat the oven to 170°C, fan 150°C, gas mark 3½ and line 2 baking trays with baking paper. In a large bowl, combine 275g **porridge oats**, 70g **flaked almonds** and ½ teaspoon **salt**. Stir in 100g **clear honey**, 60ml **vegetable oil** and 1 teaspoon **vanilla extract**, folding the mixture until the dry ingredients are completely coated. Spoon onto the prepared baking trays and spread out in an even layer. Bake for 15 minutes, then add 4 tablespoons **pumpkin seeds** and stir. Cook for another 10 minutes, or until golden (it will crisp up as it cools). Set aside to cool completely, then stir through 50g **puffed rice cereal**. Store the granola in an airtight container for up to 2 weeks. Serve with **0% fat natural Greek yogurt** and **fresh fruit** of your choice, such as blueberries.

6 SmartPoints value per serving

Spring mains

Primavera risotto

serves 4   prep time 25 minutes   cook time 45 minutes

A classic Italian-style spring vegetable and rice dish – our simple version includes fresh asparagus, pesto and broad beans.

200g frozen broad beans
Calorie controlled cooking spray
3 shallots, finely chopped
300g Arborio rice
80ml white wine
1.4 litres hot vegetable stock, made with 2 stock cubes
250g asparagus, roughly chopped
30g reduced-fat green pesto
80g vegetarian Italian-style hard cheese, finely grated
Finely grated zest of ½ lemon, plus lemon wedges to serve
1 tablespoon finely chopped fresh basil

1   Cook the beans in boiling water for 2 minutes, until just tender. Drain, then refresh in cold water and drain again. Remove and discard the skins from the beans, then set aside. Mist a large nonstick pan with cooking spray and put over a medium heat. Add the shallots and cook for 5-6 minutes until soft, then stir in the rice and cook for 2 minutes.

2   Add the wine and gently simmer for 1 minute, then pour in a ladleful of the stock. Cook, stirring constantly, until the stock has been almost completely absorbed by the rice. Repeat until all the stock has been used, adding the asparagus and broad beans with the final ladleful. Cook for 5 minutes, or until the asparagus is al dente. The whole process should take about 30 minutes.

3   Season well, then stir in the pesto, most of the grated cheese, half the lemon zest and the chopped basil. Serve with the remaining cheese and zest scattered over, with the lemon wedges on the side.

12   **SmartPoints value per serving**

Cook's tip
Use frozen peas instead of broad beans if you have them to hand for no extra SmartPoints.

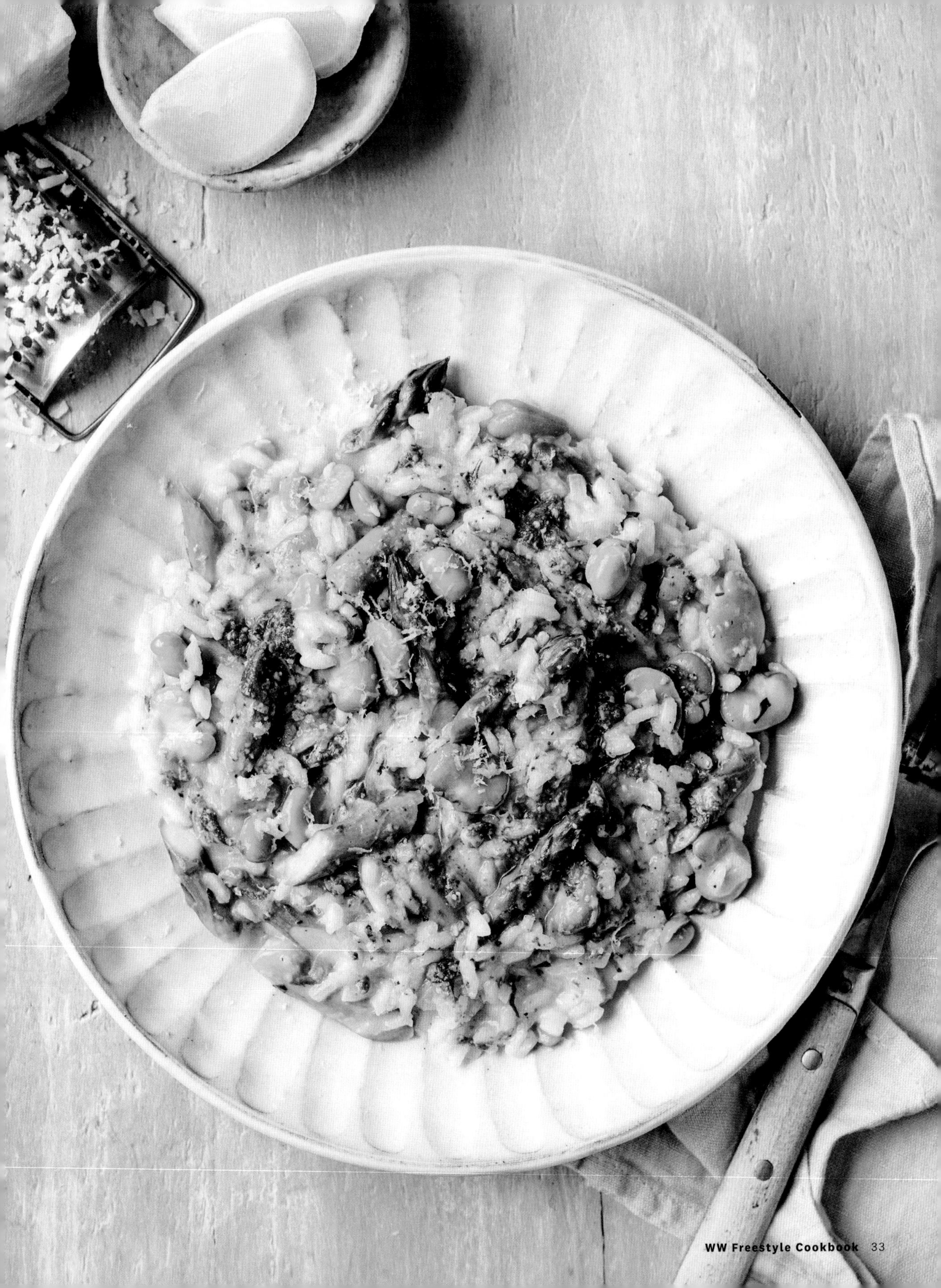

Courgette & turkey lasagne

serves 4   prep time 10 minutes   cook time 55 minutes

Forget pasta sheets – this simple and fresh lasagne layers a delicious turkey mince ragù with thin slices of courgette and creamy mascarpone cheese.

Calorie controlled cooking spray
1 onion, finely chopped
2 garlic cloves, crushed
500g turkey breast mince
2 x 400g tins chopped tomatoes
½ tablespoon dried oregano
1 tablespoon finely chopped fresh basil
½ tablespoon balsamic vinegar
600g courgettes
200g light mascarpone
25g Parmesan, grated
400g new potatoes, halved
2 tablespoons chopped fresh flat-leaf parsley

1 Mist a large nonstick pan with cooking spray and set over a low heat, then add the onion and cook for 6-8 minutes until soft. Add the garlic and cook for a further 1 minute. Add the mince and cook, stirring, for 2-3 minutes, until it starts to brown, then add the tomatoes, oregano, basil and balsamic vinegar. Season to taste, then stir to combine. Simmer, uncovered, for 20 minutes, until the sauce has reduced.

2 Meanwhile, use a vegetable peeler to slice the courgettes into thin strips. Preheat the oven to 200°C, fan 180°C, gas mark 6.

3 Pour one-third of the turkey ragù into a 20cm x 20cm baking dish and spoon over one-third of the mascarpone, spreading it out with a spatula. Top with a layer of the sliced courgette, then repeat twice using the remaining ragù, mascarpone and courgette. Mist the top of the lasagne with cooking spray, then scatter over the Parmesan and some freshly ground black pepper. Bake for 25 minutes until golden and bubbling, then allow to stand for 5 minutes before serving.

4 Cook the new potatoes in a pan of boiling water for 15 minutes until tender, then scatter over the parsley and serve with the lasagne.

8   **SmartPoints value per serving**

Cook's tip
To make in advance, prepare the lasagne up to the point of baking and chill in the fridge for up to 24 hours, then bake as in step 3.

Green bean, pasta, ham & egg salad

serves 4**prep time 10 minutes****cook time 15 minutes**

Pasta salad makes a great all-in-one lunch, perfect for packing into a lunch box and taking to work. Keep the dressing in a separate container until you're ready to eat.

200g small pasta shells

150g frozen peas

150g green beans

4 eggs

1½ tablespoons snipped fresh chives, plus extra to serve

½ tablespoon extra virgin olive oil

½ teaspoon Dijon mustard

Grated zest and juice of ½ lemon

100g ham, roughly chopped

1   Cook the pasta to pack instructions, adding the peas and beans for the final 4 minutes of cooking time. Drain, then transfer the pasta and vegetables to a large serving bowl.

2   Meanwhile, cook the eggs in a large pan of boiling water for 8 minutes, then drain and fill the pan with cold water. Allow the eggs to cool in the water for 5 minutes, then peel and cut into quarters. Set aside.

3   Combine the chives, olive oil, mustard and lemon zest and juice in a small jug, then drizzle over the pasta mixture and toss to combine.

4   Toss the ham through the pasta salad, then top with the eggs and the extra snipped fresh chives to serve.

6   **SmartPoints value per serving**

On the go

'With a daughter at primary school and a busy job, packed lunches that keep you feeling full all afternoon are great. Not only do they help with our healthy-eating goals, they save money, too.' **NADINE**

Chicken schnitzels with lemon & parsley potatoes

serves 4   prep time 20 minutes   cook time 15 minutes

This is a family-friendly recipe that also tastes great served cold. If you don't have panko breadcrumbs, you could use ordinary wholemeal breadcrumbs instead.

700g new potatoes, quartered

3 tablespoons plain flour

2 eggs, lightly beaten

90g panko breadcrumbs

Grated zest and juice of 1 lemon, plus lemon wedges to serve

4 x 165g skinless chicken breast fillets

Calorie controlled cooking spray

3 tablespoons reduced-fat mayonnaise

3 tablespoons finely chopped fresh parsley, plus extra leaves to serve

½ teaspoon Dijon mustard

1   Cook the potatoes in a pan of boiling water for 20 minutes or until tender, then drain.

2   Line a baking tray with baking paper and place a wire rack on top. Preheat the oven to 200°C, fan 180°C, gas mark 6. Put the flour, eggs and breadcrumbs into 3 separate shallow bowls and mix the lemon zest into the breadcrumbs. Put the chicken fillets between two pieces of nonstick baking paper and bash with a rolling pin until the chicken is about 1cm thick.

3   Dip each of the chicken fillets in the flour, then the egg and finally the breadcrumbs. Mist a large pan with cooking spray and cook for 1 minute each side until golden, then transfer to the wire rack on the baking tray and cook in the oven for 10 minutes.

4   Meanwhile, in a small jug, mix the mayonnaise, lemon juice, parsley and mustard together, and toss with the drained potatoes. Serve the potatoes alongside the schnitzel with the lemon wedges, and the extra parsley scattered over.

8   **SmartPoints value per serving**

Cook's tip
Try serving this with the Shaved green salad with hazelnuts, p63, for an extra 3 SmartPoints per serving.

Roast salmon with za'atar

serves 4 **prep time 10 minutes** **cook time 45 minutes**

This simple dish is packed with flavour. Za'atar is a blend of spices and sesame seeds that's nutty and fragrant. Plus, slow-roasting the fish keeps it tender and succulent.

1 tablespoon za'atar

Grated zest of ½ lemon

4 x 120g skinless, boneless salmon fillets

800g new potatoes, quartered

Calorie controlled cooking spray

1 teaspoon ground cumin

½ teaspoon chilli powder, plus extra to serve

Small handful fresh flat-leaf parsley leaves, to serve

1 Preheat the oven to 200°C, fan 180°C, gas mark 6. Sprinkle the za'atar and lemon zest over the salmon and rub in to coat, then set aside.

2 Mist the potatoes with cooking spray, season well and toss together with the cumin and chilli powder. Put in a roasting tin and roast for 25 minutes.

3 Stir the potatoes, then put the salmon fillets on top and cook for another 20 minutes. Scatter over the parsley leaves and sprinkle over the extra chilli powder, then serve.

5 SmartPoints value per serving

Essential eating

'As a dietitian, I'm all for any dish that includes fish. It's packed with protein and vitamins, and salmon is an excellent source of omega-3 fats which are essential nutrients and the reason why fish has its reputation as "food for the brain.' **TONY**

WW Freestyle Cookbook 41

Lamb koftas with Turkish salad

serves 4   prep time 15 minutes   cook time 15 minutes

Pitta breads are torn then toasted and tossed through salad in this easy and delicious Middle Eastern-style dish. A sprinkling of sumac gives it a citrussy tang.

2 wholemeal pitta breads
400g 10% fat lamb mince
1 teaspoon ground cumin
1 teaspoon ground coriander
¼ teaspoon ground cinnamon
2 garlic cloves, crushed
2 tablespoons finely chopped fresh flat-leaf parsley
Calorie controlled cooking spray
2 Little Gem lettuces, shredded
150g cherry tomatoes, quartered
50g light feta, crumbled
½ teaspoon sumac, plus extra to serve
Juice of ½ lemon

1   Preheat the oven to 200°C, fan 180°C, gas mark 6. Tear the pitta breads into 3-4cm pieces and put on a baking tray. Bake for 10-15 minutes until crisp and golden, then set aside.

2   In a large bowl, combine the lamb, spices, garlic and half of the parsley and season to taste. Form the mixture into 12 oval-shaped patties. If you like, you can put the koftas on metal or wooden skewers to make them easier to turn while cooking.

3   Mist a large nonstick frying pan with cooking spray and put over a medium heat. Add the lamb koftas and cook for 12-14 minutes, turning occasionally, until browned and cooked through.

4   Put the lettuce, remaining parsley, tomatoes and feta on a serving plate. In a small bowl, combine the sumac and lemon juice, then drizzle over the salad. Add the pitta bread pieces and toss to combine, then serve with the koftas and the extra sumac sprinkled over the top.

7   **SmartPoints value per serving**

Cook's tip
Serve this with the Tomato & red onion salsa, p63, for no extra SmartPoints.

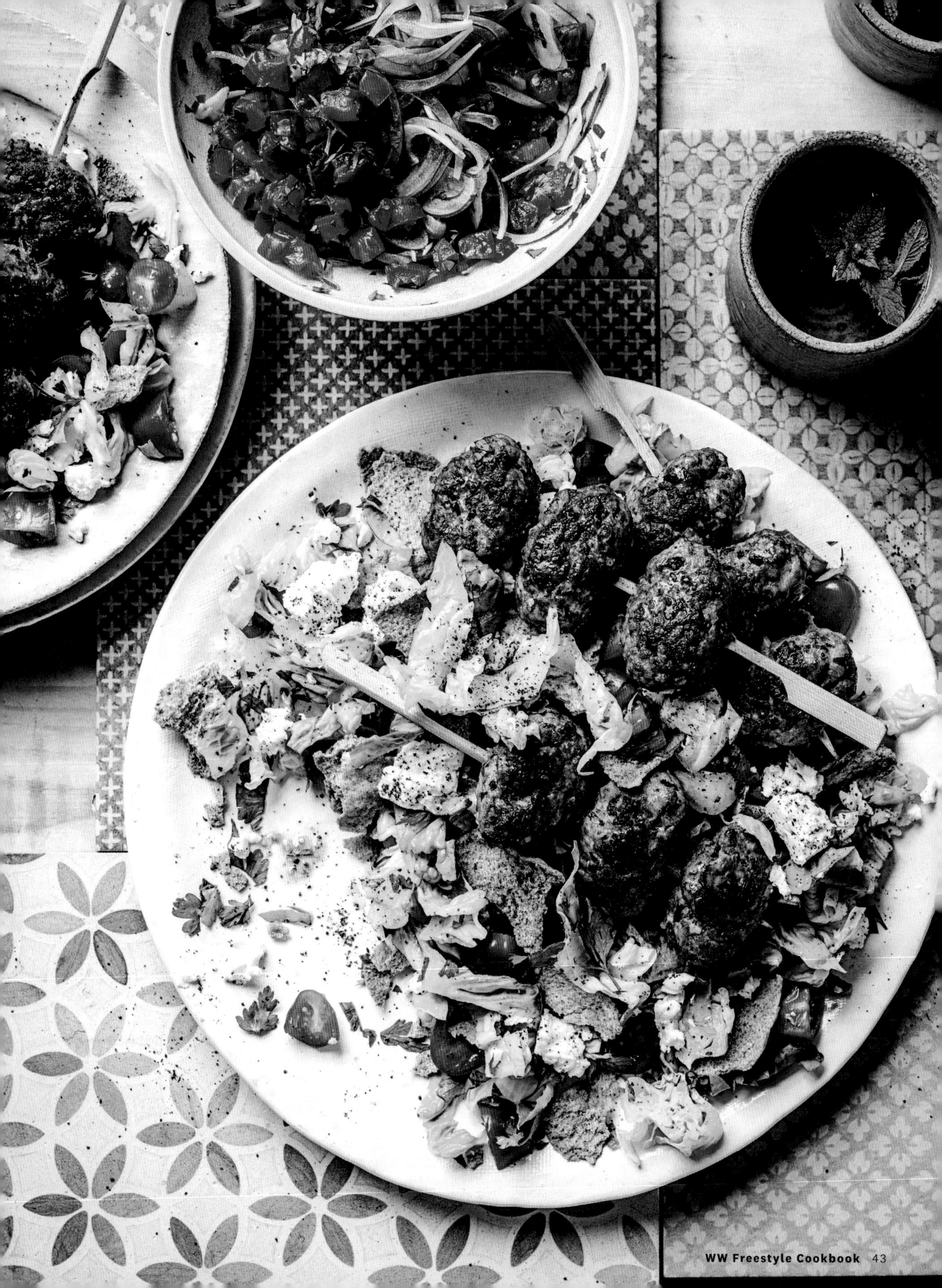

Green minestrone

serves 4   prep time 5 minutes   cook time 20 minutes

Orzo pasta, loads of vegetables and herbs, and a dollop of pesto come together in this simple soup that's bursting with spring flavours.

150g frozen broad beans

Calorie controlled cooking spray

1 shallot, finely chopped

1 celery stick, finely chopped

2 garlic cloves, crushed

1 litre vegetable stock, made with 2 stock cubes

150g orzo pasta

150g peas (frozen or fresh)

40g reduced-fat green pesto

1 tablespoon finely chopped fresh basil, plus extra leaves, to serve

Grated zest of 1 lemon

20g vegetarian Italian-style hard cheese, grated, to serve

1   Cook the beans in boiling water for 2 minutes, until just tender. Drain, then refresh in cold water and drain again. Remove and discard the skins from the beans, then set aside. Mist a large nonstick pan with cooking spray and set over a medium heat. Add the shallot and celery and cook for 6-8 minutes until soft. Add the garlic and cook for another 1 minute.

2   Pour in the stock and bring to a gentle simmer, then add the orzo pasta and cook for 7 minutes. Stir in the peas, broad beans and pesto, then cook for a further 4 minutes. Season to taste, then stir in the chopped basil and lemon zest and serve with extra fresh basil leaves and grated cheese scattered over.

4   **SmartPoints value per serving**

Cook's tip

This is a great recipe for using fresh peas – as a rule, peas in their pods will weigh about twice as much as when they're shelled, so for 150g of shelled peas, you'll need 300g of peas in the pod.

Chinese vegetable stir-fry

serves 4   prep time 20 minutes   cook time 10 minutes

Stir-frying is a great way to cook fresh vegetables. Keep it quick and they will stay nice and crisp, and won't lose any of their delicious flavour.

2 tablespoons soy sauce

1 tablespoon hoisin sauce

Grated zest and juice of 1 lime, plus wedges to serve

3cm piece fresh ginger, peeled and finely grated

2 garlic cloves, crushed

1 red chilli, finely chopped, plus extra sliced chilli to serve

1 tablespoon vegetable oil

1 red onion, finely sliced

2 pak choi, chopped

100g baby corn, halved lengthways

100g mangetout

2 eggs, lightly beaten

400g cooked egg noodles

2 tablespoons finely chopped fresh coriander, plus extra leaves, to serve

1   Combine the soy sauce, hoisin sauce, half of the lime juice, the ginger, garlic and chilli in a small bowl and set aside.

2   Heat the oil in a large wok or frying pan over a medium heat, then add the vegetables and stir-fry for 5 minutes until just tender. Add the sauce mixture and toss to combine.

3   Make a well in the centre of the vegetable mixture using a spatula. Pour in the eggs and cook for 2 minutes or until set, then roughly break up and stir through the stir-fry.

4   Add the noodles and stir them through the veg with the remaining lime juice, the lime zest and coriander. Scatter over the chilli slices and extra fresh coriander leaves, then serve with the lime wedges on the side for squeezing over.

6   **SmartPoints value per serving**

Quick and easy

'Stir-fries are brilliant for busy people. This is such an easy recipe so it's perfect for novice cooks and a great way to bulk up your intake of nutritious veggies.' **ELLA**

Pesto fish parcels

serves 4   **prep time 15 minutes**   **cook time 25 minutes**

In this ZeroPoints recipe, cod fillets are topped with a ready-made green pesto, then baked with lots of colourful veg in a paper parcel for maximum succulence and flavour.

2 tablespoons reduced-fat green pesto

4 x 100g skinless, boneless cod fillets

200g cherry tomatoes, halved

2 courgettes, cut into 5mm slices

1 red pepper, deseeded and cut into 3cm chunks

Small handful fresh basil leaves, to serve

Lemon wedges, to serve

1   Preheat the oven to 190°C, fan 170°C, gas mark 5. Spread the pesto over the fish and season to taste. Put a 40cm x 30cm rectangle of kitchen foil on the work surface and top with an equal-sized rectangle of baking paper.

2   Pile a quarter of all the vegetables on the paper, leaving a 3cm border at the edges, season to taste, then top with a piece of fish. Bring the paper up and over the fish and vegetables and scrunch the sides together to seal.

3   Put the parcel on a baking tray, then repeat with the remaining veg and fish to make 3 more parcels. Bake for 25 minutes, then transfer the parcels to plates. Open them up and scatter over the fresh basil and some freshly ground black pepper. Serve with the lemon wedges on the side for squeezing over.

0   SmartPoints value per serving

Cook's tip
You could serve this with the Smashed potatoes with chimichurri, p64, for an extra 5 SmartPoints per serving.

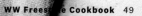

Asparagus filo quiche

serves 6   prep time 10 minutes + cooling   cook time 40 minutes

Crisp, delicate filo pastry is filled with a delicious medley of green vegetables, fresh herbs and Cheddar cheese for a simple springtime lunch or light dinner.

Calorie controlled cooking spray

9 sheets filo pastry

350g asparagus, trimmed

4 eggs, lightly beaten

250ml skimmed milk

2 spring onions, trimmed and finely sliced

150g frozen peas, defrosted

50g half-fat Cheddar cheese, grated

½ tablespoon finely chopped fresh flat-leaf parsley

½ tablespoon snipped fresh chives

½ tablespoon finely chopped fresh mint, plus extra leaves, to serve

1   Preheat the oven to 180°C, fan 160°C, gas mark 4. Mist a 22cm-round cake tin with cooking spray. Mist a sheet of filo pastry with additional cooking spray and line the tin with it. Repeat with the remaining sheets of pastry.

2   Bring a pan of water to a boil and cook the asparagus for 3 minutes, until just tender, then drain and cut into 3cm lengths.

3   In a large bowl, combine the eggs and milk, then add the asparagus, spring onions, peas, cheese and herbs and season to taste. Spoon the mixture into the filo case and bake for 30 minutes, or until just set. Allow to cool for 15 minutes. Serve with the extra herbs scattered over the top.

7 **SmartPoints value per serving**

Cook's tip
Try serving this with the Lemon, garlic & chilli broccoli, p63, for no extra SmartPoints per serving.

Pea & potato fritters with poached eggs

serves 4　**prep time 15 minutes**　**cook time 35 minutes**

These delicious fritters are flavoured with fresh chives and parsley, and topped with a soft poached egg. The flavours are light and delicate – perfect for spring.

500g Maris Piper potatoes, cut into small chunks

300g frozen peas

5 eggs

1 tablespoon snipped fresh chives

1 tablespoon finely chopped fresh flat-leaf parsley

2 tablespoons plain flour

Calorie controlled cooking spray

1 tablespoon white wine vinegar

100g green salad leaves, to serve

1　Put the potatoes in a medium pan of boiling water and cook for 15-20 minutes until tender, adding the peas for the final 2 minutes. Drain and roughly mash the potatoes and peas together. Preheat the oven to 180°C, fan 160°C, gas mark 4.

2　Combine the potato and pea mash, 1 egg, the herbs and flour in a large bowl and season to taste. Form the mixture into 8 patties. Mist a large nonstick frying pan with cooking spray, add 4 of the patties and cook for 2 minutes each side. Transfer to a baking tray and keep warm, then repeat to make 4 more fritters.

3　Bring a deep pan of water to a boil and add the white wine vinegar. Break 1 egg into a ramekin. Swirl the water with a spoon to create a whirlpool and slide in the egg. Cook for 2-3 minutes, then using a slotted spoon, transfer to a plate lined with kitchen paper. Repeat with the remaining 3 eggs.

4　Serve 2 fritters per person, and top with a poached egg. Season to taste and serve with the salad on the side.

The uncooked patties can be frozen in an airtight container for up to 3 months.

4　**SmartPoints value per serving**

Family favourite

'This recipe has gone down a treat in my house. You can get ahead by mixing the fritter ingredients together, forming into patties, then keeping covered in the fridge for up to 12 hours before frying.'
NADINE

Blackened chicken & Jersey Royal traybake

serves 4   prep time 15 + marinating   cook time 35 minutes

Spring is peak season for Jersey Royals. The full-flavoured potatoes are famous the world over. Try them in this Caribbean-style chicken traybake that makes a great family supper.

2 teaspoons smoked paprika

1 teaspoon ground allspice

1 teaspoon dried oregano

4 x 165g skinless chicken breast fillets

1½ tablespoons vegetable oil

750g Jersey Royal potatoes, halved and quartered

2 red onions, cut into thin wedges

1 red and 1 yellow pepper, deseeded and roughly chopped

2 garlic cloves

Calorie controlled cooking spray

Large handful fresh flat-leaf parsley, roughly chopped

1   Combine the paprika, allspice and oregano in a small bowl. Put the chicken in a food bag, season to taste, and add the spice and herb mixture and ½ tablespoon of the oil. Seal the bag and shake to coat the chicken. Transfer to the fridge to marinate for 30 minutes.

2   Preheat the oven to 200°C, fan 180°C, gas mark 6. Put the potatoes, onions, peppers and whole garlic cloves in a large roasting tin and drizzle over the remaining oil. Season to taste, then toss to combine. Roast for 20 minutes.

3   Meanwhile, mist a large nonstick pan with cooking spray and put over a medium-high heat. Add the chicken and cook for 2-3 minutes each side until charred. Transfer the chicken to the roasting tin with the potatoes and veg. Cook for another 15 minutes or until the chicken and potatoes are cooked through. Serve with the parsley scattered over the top.

6   **SmartPoints value per serving**

Cook's tip

Try serving this with Griddled asparagus with lemon vinaigrette, p64, for an extra 1 SmartPoint per serving.

Lamb steaks with sticky carrots

serves 4   prep time 15 minutes + resting   cook time 50 minutes

Looking for the perfect spring lunch? This simple take on a roast lamb dinner is just the thing if you're cooking a special meal for a smaller number of people.

4 x 100g lean lamb steaks

½ tablespoon finely chopped fresh rosemary leaves

3 sprigs fresh thyme, leaves picked and roughly chopped

1 garlic clove, crushed

1 tablespoon olive oil

1 tablespoon honey

1 tablespoon balsamic vinegar

800g baby carrots, halved lengthways

2 red onions, cut into wedges

1 tablespoon roughly chopped fresh flat-leaf parsley, plus extra, to serve

Calorie controlled cooking spray

250g young leaf spinach

Small pinch ground nutmeg

1   Preheat the oven to 200°C, fan 180°C, gas mark 6. Put the lamb in a large bowl with the rosemary, thyme and garlic, then season to taste.

2   In a small bowl, combine the olive oil, honey and balsamic vinegar. Put the carrots in a large roasting tin, drizzle over the honey mixture and toss to combine. Season to taste, then add the onions and roast for 35-40 minutes, tossing halfway, until the carrots are tender and sticky. Toss through the parsley.

3   Meanwhile, mist a large nonstick frying pan with cooking spray, add the lamb and cook for 2½ minutes each side. Cover loosely with kitchen foil and set aside to rest for 5 minutes.

4   Put the spinach in a large colander and pour over a kettleful of boiling water until completely wilted. Transfer to a medium bowl and stir through the nutmeg. Serve the lamb with the carrots, onions and spinach on the side and the extra parsley scattered over.

8   **SmartPoints value per serving**

Great for entertaining

'I have a large family and we love this dish – it's easy, tasty and a real showstopper for a spring celebration. Try serving it with the Three herb rice, p64, for an extra 6 SmartPoints per serving.' **SUE**

Mexican street-style pasta salad

serves 4   prep time 10 minutes + cooling   cook time 15 minutes

Zingy lime, avocado, black beans and jalapeño – these classic Mexican ingredients combine in this super-speedy salad that's perfect for a weekday lunch.

160g macaroni

Calorie controlled cooking spray

340g tin sweetcorn, drained

1 red pepper, deseeded and diced

400g tin black beans, drained and rinsed

1 avocado, peeled, stone removed, and roughly chopped (150g prepared weight)

3 spring onions, trimmed and thinly sliced

Large handful fresh coriander, finely chopped, plus extra, to serve

1 jalapeño, deseeded and finely chopped

30g reduced-fat mayonnaise

30g 0% fat natural Greek yogurt

¼ teaspoon smoked paprika

Grated zest and juice of 1 lime

65g light feta, crumbled

1 Cook the pasta in a pan of boiling water to pack instructions. Drain, then rinse under cold running water. Drain again and set aside.

2 Meanwhile, mist a large nonstick pan with cooking spray and put over a high heat. Add the sweetcorn and pepper and cook for 6-8 minutes, stirring occasionally, until they begin to char. Remove from the heat, season to taste and set aside to cool.

3 Put the pasta, sweetcorn and pepper mixture, the black beans, avocado, spring onions, coriander and jalapeño in a large bowl and stir to combine.

4 Combine the mayonnaise, yogurt, smoked paprika and the lime zest and juice in a small bowl, and season to taste. Drizzle over the pasta salad and toss to combine.

5 Scatter the feta and extra coriander over the pasta salad, then serve.

8   **SmartPoints value per serving**

Honey & ginger chicken stir-fry

serves 4   prep time 20 minutes   cook time 15 minutes

A simple stir-fry packed with classic Asian flavours – ginger, honey and soy – plus tender chunks of chicken and lots of fresh vegetables and herbs.

5cm piece fresh ginger, peeled and grated

2 tablespoons clear honey

1 tablespoon soy sauce

½ tablespoon sriracha sauce

2 garlic cloves, crushed

Juice of 1 lime, plus wedges to serve

4 x 165g skinless chicken breast fillets, diced

Calorie controlled cooking spray

1 carrot, peeled and cut into thin strips using a vegetable peeler

1 broccoli, cut into small florets

2 tablespoons finely chopped fresh coriander

2 x 250g pouches microwave brown basmati rice

1   Put the ginger, honey, soy sauce, sriracha, garlic and lime juice in a large bowl and whisk to combine. Add the chicken and toss to coat in the marinade. Set aside.

2   Mist a large nonstick pan or wok with cooking spray, add the carrot and broccoli and cook over a high heat for 4-5 minutes until tender, then transfer to a plate and set aside.

3   Mist the pan with more cooking spray, add the chicken and any remaining marinade and stir-fry for 5-6 minutes, until golden and cooked through. Return the vegetables to the pan to heat through, then remove from the heat and stir in the coriander.

4   Cook the rice to pack instructions. Serve the stir-fry with the rice and lime wedges on the side.

8   **SmartPoints value per serving**

Cook's tip

In a hurry? Use a ready-prepared pack of stir-fry vegetables instead of the carrot and broccoli for no extra SmartPoints.

Spring sides

Springtime means lots of fresh, crisp green veg – make the most of them with these deliciously easy side dishes.

Lemon, garlic & chilli broccoli

serves 4
prep time 10 minutes   cook time 20 minutes

Preheat the oven to 190°C, fan 170°C, gas mark 5. Put 600g **Tenderstem broccoli** in a roasting tin and toss with the juice of ½ **lemon**, 6 thinly sliced **garlic cloves** and 1 deseeded and finely chopped **red chilli**. Mist the mixture with **calorie controlled cooking spray**. Season to taste and scatter over 1 teaspoon **chilli flakes**. Cook for 15 minutes until tender. Serve with the grated zest of ½ **lemon** scattered over the top.

0   SmartPoints value per serving

Shaved green salad with hazelnuts

serves 4
prep time 15 minutes   cook time 8 minutes

Preheat the oven to 200°C, fan 180°C, gas mark 6. Put 30g blanched **hazelnuts** on a baking tray and cook for 7-8 minutes until golden, then roughly chop. In a small jug, combine 2 teaspoons **extra virgin olive oil**, ½ tablespoon **lemon juice**, ½ teaspoon **Dijon mustard**, 1 crushed **garlic clove** and 1 tablespoon cold water to make a dressing. Season to taste. Trim 2 **courgettes** and slice into ribbons with a vegetable peeler. Trim and finely chop 2 **celery sticks**, reserving the leaves. Trim and thinly slice 2 **fennel** bulbs, reserving the fronds. Put the courgette, celery, fennel and 60g **rocket** in a serving bowl and toss through the dressing. Stir in 30g shaved **vegetarian Italian-style hard cheese** and the hazelnuts, then serve with the reserved celery leaves and fennel fronds scattered over.

3   SmartPoints value per serving

Tomato & red onion salsa

serves 4
prep time 10 minutes

Halve and deseed 3 large **tomatoes**, then finely chop the flesh. Combine the tomatoes with 1 thinly sliced **red onion**, 1 deseeded and chopped **red chilli**, 2 tablespoons finely chopped **fresh coriander** and the juice of ½ **lime** in a small bowl, then season to taste and serve with extra finely chopped **fresh coriander** sprinkled over the top.

0   SmartPoints value per serving

Spring sides

Three-herb rice

serves 4
prep time 5 minutes   cook time 15 minutes

Combine 2 tablespoons each finely chopped **fresh flat-leaf parsley** and **fresh coriander**, 1 tablespoon finely chopped **fresh tarragon**, the grated zest of ½ **lemon**, 1 small crushed **garlic clove**, ½ small finely chopped **red onion** and ½ tablespoon **olive oil** in a small bowl and season to taste. Cook 200g **white basmati rice** to pack instructions, then stir through the dressing and serve with extra chopped **fresh tarragon** scattered over.

6 SmartPoints value per serving

Griddled asparagus with lemon vinaigrette

serves 4
prep time 5 minutes   cook time 4 minutes

Whisk together 2 teaspoons **olive oil**, ½ tablespoon **lemon juice**, 1 teaspoon **Dijon mustard** and 1 teaspoon **clear honey**. Put 500g trimmed **asparagus** in a large bowl and mist with **calorie controlled cooking spray**. Heat a griddle pan over a high heat until smoking, then cook the asparagus for 3-4 minutes, turning, until tender; you may need to do this in batches. Drizzle over the dressing to serve.

1 SmartPoints value per serving

Smashed potatoes with chimichurri

serves 4
prep time 10 minutes   cook time 40 minutes

Preheat the oven to 220°C, fan 200°C, gas mark 7. Cook 800g **new potatoes** in a pan of boiling water for 20 minutes, or until tender. Drain and put on a baking tray, then gently crush using the back of a spoon. Season to taste and mist with **calorie controlled cooking spray**. Roast for 20 minutes, until the edges are golden. Meanwhile, put a small handful each **fresh coriander** and **fresh flat-leaf parsley**, 1 **garlic clove**, the juice of ½ **lemon**, ½ roughly chopped small **red onion**, ½ tablespoon **olive oil**, ½ deseeded **red chilli** and ½ teaspoon **white wine vinegar** in a mini food processor with 1 tablespoon cold water, then blitz to combine. Spoon the chimichurri over the potatoes and serve.

5 SmartPoints value per serving

Spring snacks & desserts

This time of year calls for bright, fresh flavours, whether you fancy something sweet or savoury.

Cinnamon crepes with griddled bananas

serves 4
prep time 5 minutes   cook time 20 minutes

Preheat the oven to 150°C, fan 130°C, gas mark 2. Sift 60g **wholemeal flour**, ¼ teaspoon **salt** and ½ teaspoon **ground cinnamon** into a bowl. In a separate bowl, combine 1 **egg** and 150ml **skimmed milk**, then whisk the egg mixture into the flour mixture. Mist a nonstick pan with **calorie controlled cooking spray** and set over a medium heat. Add a quarter of the batter, then tilt the pan until the base is coated. Cook for 2 minutes, then flip and cook for another 1 minute. Transfer the crepe to a baking tray and keep warm in the oven. Repeat to make 4 crepes, keeping them separated on the baking tray with nonstick baking paper. Heat a griddle pan over a high heat until just smoking. Halve 4 **bananas** lengthways and mist with cooking spray, then griddle for 2 minutes on each side until lightly charred. Cut into pieces. Top the crepes with the bananas, then fold in half and drizzle over 1 tablespoon **clear honey** between the 4 pancakes. Serve each with 25g **0% fat natural Greek yogurt**, with extra **ground cinnamon** sprinkled over the top.

3 SmartPoints value per serving

Spring snacks & desserts

Houmous with crudités

serves 4
prep time 10 minutes

Put a 400g tin rinsed and drained **chickpeas** in a mini food processor with 40g **tahini**, 2 teaspoons **olive oil**, 100g **0% fat natural Greek yogurt**, 1 small crushed **garlic clove** and the juice of ½ **lemon**, then blitz to a coarse purée. Season to taste, then add 1 tablespoon cold water and blitz again. Transfer to a serving bowl and sprinkle over ¼ teaspoon **ground cumin**, then serve with 80g trimmed **chicory leaves**, 80g halved **baby corn**, 1 deseeded and sliced **red pepper** and 100g trimmed **heritage carrots**.

3 SmartPoints value per serving

Carrot cake snack bites

makes 25
prep time 20 minutes
+ soaking and chilling

Put 12 pitted **medjool dates** in a large bowl, cover with hot water and set aside to soak for 10 minutes, until slightly softened. Drain, then transfer to a food processor. Add 50g **porridge oats**, 50g roughly chopped **pecans**, 70g grated **carrot**, 1 tablespoon **chia seeds**, and 1 teaspoon each of **ground ginger**, **ground cinnamon** and **vanilla extract**. Blitz until smooth, then transfer to the fridge to chill for 30 minutes. Roll the chilled mixture into 25 balls using a small spoon, then roll in 25g desiccated **coconut** to serve. The bites will keep in the fridge in an airtight container for 3-4 days.

1 SmartPoints value per bite

Chocolate courgette loaf cake

makes 10 slices
prep time 15 minutes
cook time 45 minutes

Preheat the oven to 180°C, fan 160°C, gas mark 4. Grease an 800g loaf tin with 1 teaspoon **low-fat spread** and line the base with baking paper. Put 30g **dark chocolate** and 50g **low-fat spread** in a heatproof bowl set over a pan of simmering water. Stir until melted. Transfer the mixture to a large bowl and add 2 **eggs**, 150g **golden caster sugar**, 150g grated **courgette**, 1 teaspoon **vanilla extract**, 120g **self-raising flour**, 2 tablespoons **cocoa powder** and 1 teaspoon **baking powder**, then beat together with a wooden spoon. Pour the batter into the loaf tin and level the top using a spatula. Bake for 45 minutes, or until a skewer inserted into the centre of the cake comes out clean. Sprinkle over 1 teaspoon **cocoa powder** to serve. The cake will keep in an airtight container for up to 4 days.

7 SmartPoints value per slice

Mango, lime & yogurt ice lollies

makes 6
prep time 10 minutes + freezing

Put 2 roughly chopped **mangos**, peeled and stones removed, in a mini food processor with the grated zest of 2 **limes** and blitz until smooth. Put 250g **0% fat natural Greek yogurt** and 4 tablespoons **clear honey** in a bowl and stir to combine, then gently fold the mango mixture through the yogurt mixture until it is swirled, but not fully combined. Spoon the mixture into 6 x 75ml ice lolly moulds. Poke a lolly stick into each mould, then freeze for 6 hours or until frozen.

2 SmartPoints value per lolly

Summer

Sunny

Sunny and warm or a bit cloudy – whatever the weather, summer means barbecues, laid-back get-togethers and al fresco dining. Think easy, fuss-free meals, thrown-together salads, quick picnic snacks and simple desserts made with gorgeously fresh ingredients. And because there's a bumper crop of fruit and veg, from sweet strawberries to juicy tomatoes, there's no end of recipe inspiration, no matter what you're after. So bring on the fruit salads, homemade burgers and on-the-go frittatas, it's time to celebrate summer!

'My favourite thing about summer is the chance to eat al fresco, while the sun is out and there's warmth in the air.'

ELISHA

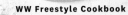

Summer breakfasts

Start your day with a little sunshine! These bright breakfasts and brunches are bursting with seasonal flavours, ripe fruits and delicious veg.

Tropical fruit salad with oats & yogurt

serves 4
prep time 10 minutes   **cook time 2 minutes**

Toast 40g **porridge oats** and 10g **desiccated coconut** in a pan over a medium heat for 2 minutes until golden, then remove from the heat. Put 300g peeled and sliced **mango**, 2 peeled and sliced **kiwi fruit**, the pulp and seeds from 1 **passion fruit** and 2 tablespoons **freshly squeezed orange juice** in a bowl and stir in 1 tablespoon chopped **fresh mint**. Combine 250g **Alpro Plain with Coconut yogurt alternative**, 250g **Alpro Simply Plain yogurt alternative** and ½ tablespoon **freshly squeezed orange juice**. Serve the yogurt mixture with the fruit spooned over, and the oats and extra **fresh mint leaves** scattered over.

3 SmartPoints value per serving

Spicy Mexican beans & avocado on toast

serves 4
prep time 10 minutes
cook time 35 minutes

Mist a medium lidded nonstick pan with **calorie controlled cooking spray** and cook ½ finely chopped **red onion** for 6-8 minutes over a medium heat until soft. Stir in 1 crushed **garlic clove**, ½ tablespoon **smoked paprika**, ½ tablespoon **ground cumin** and ½ teaspoon **chilli powder**, and cook for another minute. Stir in 1 tablespoon **tomato purée**. Add 2 x 400g tins drained and rinsed **kidney beans**, a 400g tin **chopped tomatoes** and 2 tablespoons water and simmer, covered, for 15 minutes, then remove the lid and cook for another 10 minutes, until thickened. Season to taste. In a small bowl, combine 2 tablespoons finely chopped **fresh coriander** with the grated zest and juice of 1 **lime**. Toast 4 slices **WW Malted Danish Bread**, then top with the beans and 150g thinly sliced **avocado**. Drizzle over the coriander dressing. Serve with extra **chilli powder** and **fresh coriander leaves** sprinkled over, with **lime wedges** on the side.

4 SmartPoints value per serving

Cook's tip
Soak the oats
overnight if you
can – it will make
the muesli softer
and creamier.

Pancakes with bacon & bananas

serves 4
prep time 5 minutes
cook time 15 minutes

Put 130g **wholemeal flour**,
1 teaspoon **baking powder** and
a pinch of **salt** in a bowl and stir to
combine. Combine 1 lightly beaten
egg and 180ml **sweetened almond
milk** in a separate bowl, then
stir into the dry ingredients until
combined. Put a large nonstick pan
over a medium heat and mist with
calorie controlled cooking spray.
Pour 4 spoonfuls of batter into the
pan; each should be about 9cm
in diameter. Cook for 1½ minutes
until bubbles form on the surface,
then flip and cook for a further
1½ minutes. Transfer to a plate
and repeat to make 12 pancakes.
Mist a large nonstick pan with
cooking spray and fry 8 **unsmoked
bacon medallions** for 2 minutes
each side until golden. Thinly slice
2 **bananas**. Stack 3 pancakes
together per serving, alternating
layers of banana and bacon
between them, then drizzle
½ tablespoon **maple syrup**
over each serving to serve.

Bircher muesli with peaches

serves 4
prep time 10 minutes + chilling

Roughly chop 2 ripe **peaches**, stones removed, then put
in a mini food processor and blitz until smooth. Put 350ml
unsweetened almond milk, 150g **porridge oats**, ½ teaspoon
vanilla extract, 250g **fat-free natural yogurt** and the peach
purée in a large bowl and stir to combine. Cover with clingfilm,
then chill in the fridge for 4 hours or overnight. To serve, divide
the muesli between 4 bowls and top with 1 sliced **peach**, stone
removed, 15g toasted **flaked almonds** and 2 teaspoons **clear
honey**, divided between the 4 bowls.

6 SmartPoints value per serving

6 SmartPoints value per serving

Summer mains

Chicken & halloumi skewers

serves 4   prep time 25 minutes + marinating   cook time 15 minutes

Even if the sun doesn't come out, these skewers will make a great 'barbecued' meal – simply cook indoors under the grill for the same tasty flavour.

Grated zest and juice of ½ lemon

½ tablespoon extra virgin olive oil

4 sprigs fresh thyme, leaves picked

1 red chilli, deseeded and finely chopped

2 x 165g skinless chicken breast fillets, cut into chunks

220g light halloumi, cubed

1 red pepper, deseeded and cut into chunks

1 courgette, cut into chunks

200g fat-free natural yogurt

1 tablespoon harissa paste

60g rocket, to serve

1   Soak 4 wooden skewers in a shallow dish of cold water for at least 10 minutes. Set aside. Put the lemon zest and juice, olive oil, thyme leaves and chilli in a small jug and whisk to combine.

2   Put the chicken, halloumi, pepper and courgette in a medium bowl, drizzle over the marinade and stir to combine, then cover with clingfilm and chill in the fridge for 2 hours.

3   Heat the grill to high. Thread the marinated ingredients onto the skewers, then grill for 10 minutes, turning halfway through, until the chicken is golden and cooked through.

4   Put the yogurt and harissa paste in small bowl and stir to combine. Serve the skewers with the harissa yogurt drizzled over, with the rocket leaves on the side.

5   SmartPoints value per serving

Cook's tip
You could serve this with a 2-ingredient flatbread per person, p110, for an extra 3 SmartPoints per serving.

Vietnamese beef noodle salad

serves 4   prep time 30 minutes   cook time 10 minutes

This bright salad packs in plenty of fresh veg, which makes a brilliant ZeroPoint ingredient base for perfectly cooked steak and a zesty lime and ginger dressing.

500g sirloin steak, fat trimmed
Calorie controlled cooking spray
200g vermicelli rice noodles
1 tablespoon fish sauce
1 tablespoon soy sauce
Grated zest and juice of 1 lime
3cm piece fresh ginger, peeled and finely grated
1 red chilli, deseeded and finely chopped
½ cucumber, cut into matchsticks
1 carrot, cut into matchsticks
6 plum tomatoes, quartered
Small handful fresh coriander, roughly chopped
Small handful fresh mint, roughly chopped

1   Put the steak on a plate, set out on the work surface and allow to come to room temperature. Season to taste. Put a nonstick frying pan over a high heat and mist with cooking spray. Add the steak and cook for 3-4 minutes each side. Transfer to a clean plate and leave to rest for 10 minutes, then slice into thin strips.

2   Cook the vermicelli noodles to pack instructions. Put the fish sauce, soy sauce, lime zest and juice, ginger and chilli in a small jug and stir to combine.

3   Put the steak, noodles, cucumber, carrot, tomatoes and fresh herbs in a serving bowl, pour over the dressing and toss everything together to combine, then serve.

8   SmartPoints value per serving

Asian flavour
'I love street food and I love the flavours of the Far East. This dish transports me straight to the bustling streets of Ho Chi Minh City.' **JONNY**

Mediterranean aubergine rolls

serves 4   **prep time 35 minutes**   **cook time 40 minutes**

Be transported to Greece – even if you're not off on holiday – with this combination of aubergines, tomatoes, olives and tangy feta cheese.

Calorie controlled cooking spray

2 large aubergines, trimmed and cut lengthways into 5mm slices

1 red onion, finely chopped

2 garlic cloves, crushed

50g pitted green olives, roughly chopped

5 tomatoes, roughly chopped

1 tablespoon tomato purée

Small handful fresh basil, roughly chopped

50g light feta, crumbled

1 tablespoon toasted pine nuts

Green salad leaves, to serve

Lemon wedges, to serve

1 Preheat the oven to 200°C, fan 180°C, gas mark 6.

2 Put a nonstick griddle over a high heat. Mist with cooking spray and griddle the aubergine slices for 2-3 minutes on each side until golden; you will need to do this in batches. Set aside.

3 Mist a nonstick pan with cooking spray and set over a medium heat. Add the onion and cook for 6-8 minutes until softened. Add the garlic and cook for another 1 minute. Remove from the heat and add the olives, tomatoes and tomato purée. Season to taste and stir through the basil.

4 Spoon 1 tablespoon of the tomato mixture over one end of each griddled aubergine slice, then roll them up. Put the rolled aubergine slices in a baking dish, seam-side down, then spoon over the remaining tomato mixture. Scatter over the feta and pine nuts. Bake for 20 minutes, until bubbling and golden, then serve with the green salad leaves and lemon wedges on the side.

2 **SmartPoints value per serving**

Cook's tip
If your aubergine rolls start to unravel, secure them with a cocktail stick and remove before serving.

Picnic frittata

serves 4   prep time 25 minutes   cook time 40 minutes

While this veggie frittata is great for al fresco meals in the park, it's also perfect for packing in lunch boxes during summer days out.

Calorie controlled cooking spray

200g new potatoes, halved

150g asparagus, trimmed

Small handful fresh basil, leaves picked and torn

5 plum tomatoes, quartered

2 spring onions, trimmed and finely sliced

8 eggs, lightly beaten

4 tablespoons ricotta cheese

10g vegetarian Italian-style hard cheese, grated

Green salad leaves, to serve

1 Preheat the oven to 200°C, fan 180°C, gas mark 6. Line a 20cm x 30cm baking tray with baking paper and mist with cooking spray.

2 Cook the potatoes in a pan of boiling water for 15-20 minutes until tender. Add the asparagus to the pan for the final 2 minutes of cooking time. Drain and set aside to cool slightly.

3 Spread the potatoes, asparagus, basil, tomatoes and spring onions in the baking tray and pour over the eggs. Spoon over the ricotta, then sprinkle over the grated cheese and season to taste.

4 Bake for 15-20 minutes, or until the egg has set completely. Set aside to cool slightly, then cut into squares. Serve hot or cold with the salad leaves on the side.

 SmartPoints value per serving

Caribbean-style salmon bowl

serves 4   prep time 15 minutes + marinating   cook time 20 minutes

This easy meal-in-a-bowl combines spicy marinated salmon fillets with basmati rice and a delicious griddled corn and tomato salad – perfect for al fresco eating.

4 x 120g skinless salmon fillets

100g jerk marinade

Calorie controlled cooking spray

2 corn cobs

150g cherry tomatoes, quartered

4 spring onions, trimmed and finely chopped

1 small red chilli, deseeded and finely chopped

Juice of 1 lime, plus wedges, to serve

200g brown basmati rice

Small handful fresh coriander, finely chopped, plus extra leaves, to serve

1   Put the salmon in a shallow dish and add the jerk marinade, turning the salmon to coat, then cover with clingfilm and chill in the fridge for 15 minutes.

2   Meanwhile, put a nonstick griddle pan over a medium-high heat and mist with cooking spray. Add the corn cobs and cook for 10 minutes, turning occasionally, until charred all over. Set aside to cool.

3   Using a sharp knife, slice the corn kernels from the cobs. Transfer to a small bowl with the tomatoes, spring onions and chilli, then add half of the lime juice, season to taste and toss to combine. Set aside.

4   Preheat the grill to medium and line a grill pan with kitchen foil. Grill the salmon, turning occasionally, for 8–10 minutes, or until the fillets are just cooked through. Break the salmon into large chunks with a fork.

5   Meanwhile, cook the rice to pack instructions. Toss the chopped coriander and remaining lime juice through the rice and divide between 4 bowls. Top with the salmon, corn salad, lime wedges and coriander leaves to serve.

5   **SmartPoints value per serving**

The perfect bowl

'I enjoy any dish that reminds me of my Caribbean heritage – and this dish is healthy and easy to prepare, too. The family love it!' **NADINE**

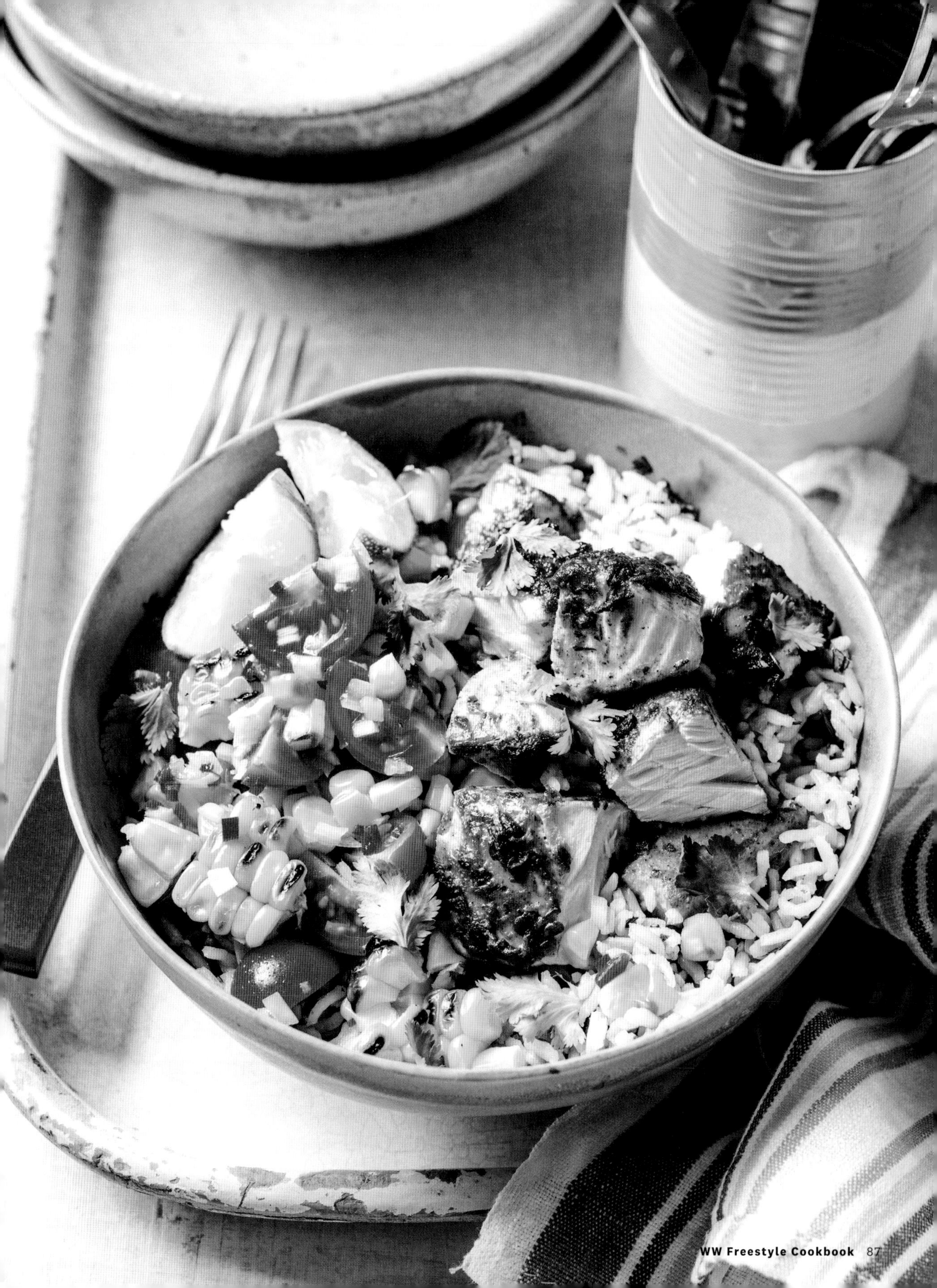

Italian chicken traybake

serves 4   prep time 15 minutes   cook time 50 minutes

Nothing says 'easy' at the end of a busy day like a traybake that you can throw together. And with sunny tomatoes, peppers and olives, it's great for this time of year.

3 x 200g baking potatoes, cut into wedges

4 tomatoes, halved

1 fennel bulb, trimmed and cut into wedges

1 red and 1 yellow pepper, both deseeded and cut into chunks

1 tablespoon dried oregano

1 lemon, halved

50g pitted black olives in brine

4 x 165g skinless chicken breast fillets

Calorie controlled cooking spray

1 tablespoon pine nuts

Small handful fresh basil, leaves torn

1   Preheat the oven to 200°C, fan 180°C, gas mark 6.

2   Bring a large lidded pan of water to a boil, add the potato wedges and simmer for 8 minutes. Drain, then return the wedges to the pan and set aside, covered, for 5 minutes to steam.

3   In a large roasting tin, combine the wedges, tomatoes, fennel, peppers, oregano, lemon and olives. Spread the mixture out into a single layer and top with the chicken breasts. Mist with cooking spray and season to taste, then roast for 40-45 minutes until the wedges are soft and the chicken is cooked through. Add the pine nuts in the final 10 minutes of cooking time.

4   Scatter over the basil and squeeze over the juice from the roasted lemon.

5 SmartPoints value per serving

Cook's tip

Make this meat-free by swapping the chicken breasts for chunks of butternut squash and cauliflower florets. The SmartPoints will be the same.

Spicy black bean burgers

serves 4   prep time 25 minutes   cook time 35 minutes

These vegan-friendly burgers are made with black beans, onion, garlic and plenty of flavourful spices – they're sure to be a hit with the whole family.

1 red onion, finely chopped

1 garlic clove, crushed

1 teaspoon smoked paprika

1 tablespoon ground coriander

Small handful fresh coriander, finely chopped

2 x 400g tins black beans, drained and rinsed

25g dry vegan breadcrumbs

Calorie controlled cooking spray

450g sweet potatoes, cut into wedges

Grated zest and juice of ½ lime

4 tablespoons Alpro Simply Plain yogurt alternative

4 x 60g seeded vegan wholemeal rolls, halved

1 cos lettuce, leaves separated

2 tomatoes, finely sliced

10-minute coleslaw, p110, to serve

1   Preheat the oven to 200°C, fan 180°C, gas mark 6. Line 2 baking trays with baking paper.

2   Put the onion, garlic, paprika, ground coriander, half of the fresh coriander, the black beans and breadcrumbs in a food processor and blitz until the mixture starts to come together; it should be chunky. Season to taste. Shape the bean mixture into 4 patties, then transfer to one of the prepared baking trays and mist with cooking spray. Put the sweet potato wedges on the second baking tray and mist with cooking spray. Bake the burgers and wedges for 30-35 minutes, turning halfway through, until the burgers are crisp and the wedges are cooked through.

3   Meanwhile, in a small jug, combine the lime zest and juice and yogurt alternative, then season to taste.

4   Put a burger on half of each roll, then top with the lettuce leaves, tomato slices and remaining coriander. Drizzle over the yogurt sauce. Serve with the sweet potato wedges and the coleslaw on the side.

The uncooked patties can be frozen in an airtight container for up to 3 months. Defrost in the fridge overnight before cooking.

9   **SmartPoints value per serving**

Take it outdoors

'Not only is this the perfect vegan barbecue alternative – it'll be a winner with your non-vegan friends and family, too!' **ELISHA**

Tuna, red onion & butter bean salad

serves 4   prep time 15 minutes + pickling   cook time 10 minutes

On warmer days, nothing beats a Zero SmartPoint salad. This one is brightened with the help of a sharp onion and lemon pickle, so there's no need for extra dressing.

1 red onion, thinly sliced

Grated zest and juice of 1 lemon

1 teaspoon caster sugar

1 teaspoon fine sea salt

Calorie controlled cooking spray

2 garlic cloves, thinly sliced

½ teaspoon chilli flakes

½ teaspoon ground coriander

400g tin butter beans, drained and rinsed

Small handful fresh flat-leaf parsley, finely chopped

2 x 160g tins tuna in spring water, drained and flaked

30g rocket

1   In a medium non-metallic bowl, combine the onion, half of the lemon juice, the caster sugar and salt and set aside for 20 minutes to pickle. When it's bright pink in colour, drain and set aside.

2   Put a large nonstick frying pan over a medium heat and mist with cooking spray. Add the garlic and cook for 2 minutes until fragrant, then add the chilli flakes and ground coriander and cook for a further 1 minute. Add the butter beans and 50ml water and simmer for 10 minutes, stirring occasionally. Lightly crush the butter beans using the back of a wooden spoon, then stir through half of the parsley. Season to taste. Stir through the remaining lemon juice and the lemon zest. Set aside to cool slightly.

3   In a large bowl, toss together the onion pickle, butter bean mixture, tuna, rocket and remaining parsley, then serve warm or cold.

0   SmartPoints value per serving

Great for sharing

'This is a brilliant salad that you can put together with mostly storecupboard ingredients when you don't feel like much cooking.'
ELLA

Pork larb

serves 4 **prep time 25 minutes** **cook time 15 minutes**

Traditional larb originated in Laos, but is now popular in many South East Asian countries. Our version uses lean pork mince and is served in crisp lettuce leaves.

Calorie controlled cooking spray

1 stem lemongrass, trimmed and tough outer layer removed, finely chopped

1 red chilli, deseeded and finely chopped

2 garlic cloves, crushed

500g 5% fat pork mince

1 tablespoon fish sauce

Grated zest and juice of 1 lime

Small handful fresh coriander, finely chopped

Small handful fresh mint, leaves picked and finely chopped

2 spring onions, trimmed and finely chopped

3 Little Gem lettuces, leaves separated

1 Set a large nonstick pan over a high heat and mist with cooking spray. Add the lemongrass, chilli and garlic and cook for 3 minutes until just starting to soften. Add the mince, breaking up any lumps, and cook for 10-12 minutes until brown. Drain any excess fat and discard.

2 Drizzle the fish sauce over the mince mixture, then stir to combine and remove from the heat. Stir through the lime zest and juice, coriander, mint and spring onions.

3 Fill 12 of the largest lettuce leaves with the mince mixture. Shred any remaining lettuce and serve on the side.

4 **SmartPoints value per serving**

Cook's tip
Serve this with the Satay noodles, p109, for an extra 7 SmartPoints per serving.

Harissa salmon & prawn parcels

serves 4   **prep time 15 minutes**   **cook time 30 minutes**

Make a fuss-free fish supper with these easy parcels – they're self-contained, which means there's less washing-up to do!

1 fennel bulb, trimmed and thinly sliced

1 red pepper, deseeded and sliced

1 courgette, sliced

8 plum tomatoes, halved

4 x 120g skinless salmon fillets

2 tablespoons rose harissa paste

200g peeled raw king prawns

1 teaspoon cumin seeds

1 lemon, quartered

4 sprigs fresh mint, leaves picked and finely chopped, to serve

1   Preheat the oven to 200°C, fan 180°C, gas mark 6. Lay 4 x 30cm baking paper squares out on the work surface.

2   Divide the fennel, pepper, courgette and tomatoes between the baking paper squares, leaving a 5cm border. Top each with a salmon fillet, then spread ½ tablespoon harissa over each fillet. Divide the prawns between the squares and sprinkle over the cumin seeds. Squeeze 1 quarter of lemon over each.

3   Bring the edges of the baking paper squares up and over the filling to create a parcel. Put on a baking tray and bake for 25-30 minutes, until the salmon is cooked through.

4   To serve, open the parcels and scatter over the mint.

1   **SmartPoints value per serving**

Cook's tip
Serve this with the Jewelled giant couscous, p110 for an extra 6 SmartPoints per serving.

Greek chicken souvlaki wrap

serves 4   prep time 20 minutes + marinating   cook time 10 minutes

These handy wraps are great for grab-and-go lunches – just prep the chicken in advance, then roll them up when you need a quick meal.

4 x 165g skinless chicken breast fillets, cut into chunks

Grated zest and juice of 1 lemon

2 teaspoons dried oregano

3 garlic cloves, crushed

Calorie controlled cooking spray

6 tablespoons fat-free natural yogurt

½ cucumber, deseeded and cut into small chunks

2 sprigs fresh mint, leaves picked and finely chopped

4 WW White Wraps

½ red onion, thinly sliced

1 cos lettuce, finely shredded

1 In a large non-metallic bowl, combine the chicken, half of the lemon zest and juice, the oregano and two-thirds of the garlic, then season to taste. Cover with clingfilm and transfer to the fridge to marinate for 2 hours, or overnight.

2 Heat the grill to high. Put the chicken on the grill tray in a single layer and mist with cooking spray. Grill for 10-12 minutes, turning halfway through, until golden and cooked through.

3 Meanwhile, in a small bowl, combine the yogurt, cucumber, mint, remaining lemon zest and juice and garlic, then season to taste.

4 Put the wraps under the grill for 10 seconds each side, then top with the chicken, red onion, lettuce and the yogurt sauce. Roll up and serve.

4 SmartPoints value per serving

Cook's tip
Serve this with the Roasted tomato & rocket salad, p109, for an extra 1 SmartPoint per serving.

Prawn pad Thai

serves 4**prep time 15 minutes****cook time 10 minutes**

This refreshing noodle dish makes the most of ZeroPoint ingredients, such as prawns and eggs, to create a light but filling meal.

240g medium rice noodles

Calorie controlled cooking spray

1 garlic clove, crushed

1 red chilli, deseeded and thinly sliced

200g peeled raw king prawns

1 egg, beaten

1 courgette, coarsely grated

1 tablespoon fish sauce

2 spring onions, trimmed and finely sliced

100g bean sprouts

2 tablespoons unsalted roasted peanuts, roughly chopped, to serve

Juice of 1 lime, plus quarters, to serve

1 Cook the noodles to pack instructions and set aside.

2 Put a wok or large nonstick frying pan over a high heat and mist with cooking spray. Add the garlic and chilli and cook for 2 minutes until fragrant, then add the prawns and cook for 1-2 minutes until they start to turn pink.

3 Push everything to one side of the pan, then add the egg and scramble, stirring with a wooden spoon.

4 Add the courgette, fish sauce, spring onions and bean sprouts, cook for 3 minutes, then add the noodles and toss to combine. Serve topped with the peanuts, the lime juice drizzled over and the lime quarters on the side.

 SmartPoints value per serving

Cook's tip

You could swap the prawns for 2 x 165g diced chicken breasts, stir-fried for 2-3 minutes until cooked through, for no extra SmartPoints.

Roasted tomato couscous with feta

serves 4   prep time 15 minutes   cook time 25 minutes

For those days you fancy a lighter meal, this bowl is a brilliant option – it's richly flavoured, thanks to the roasted tomatoes and toasted spices, and has a tangy kick from the feta.

200g cherry tomatoes, halved

2 garlic cloves, crushed

Calorie controlled cooking spray

1 teaspoon fennel seeds

1 teaspoon cumin seeds

200g couscous

400ml hot vegetable stock, made with 1 stock cube

100g light feta, crumbled

Small handful fresh basil, leaves picked and torn

400g tin chickpeas, drained and rinsed

1 iceberg lettuce, roughly chopped

Lemon wedges, to serve

1 Preheat the oven to 180°C, fan 160°C, gas mark 4. Put the cherry tomatoes, cut side up, on a baking tray and sprinkle over the garlic. Season to taste and mist with cooking spray. Roast for 25 minutes or until softened and lightly golden.

2 Meanwhile, in a small dry frying pan set over a low heat, toast the fennel and cumin seeds for 1 minute, or until fragrant.

3 Put the toasted seeds and couscous in a large bowl and pour over the stock. Cover with clingfilm and set aside for 15-20 minutes, until the couscous has absorbed all the stock. Remove the clingfilm and fluff the couscous using a fork.

4 Stir the roasted tomatoes, feta, basil and chickpeas through the couscous. Season to taste with freshly ground black pepper and serve with the lettuce on the side and the lemon wedges for squeezing over.

7 **SmartPoints value per serving**

Make it your own

'I loved this dish as a veggie, and now I'm experimenting with vegan eating, I still enjoy it – I just leave out the feta!' **SELEN**

Chicken & vegetable paella

serves 4   **freezable**   **prep time 20 minutes**   **cook time 25 minutes**

This classic entertaining dish is perfect for feeding a crowd, or simply enjoying on a warm summer weekend with the family.

Calorie controlled cooking spray

2 x 165g skinless chicken breast fillets, thinly sliced

1 red onion, roughly chopped

1 red pepper, deseeded and roughly chopped

1 carrot, finely chopped

1 tablespoon smoked paprika

300g paella rice

2 sprigs fresh thyme

400g tin chopped tomatoes

1 litre chicken stock, made with 1 stock cube

Small handful fresh flat-leaf parsley, finely chopped, to serve

Lemon halves, to serve

1   Put a large nonstick frying pan or wok over a high heat and mist with cooking spray. Add the chicken and cook, stirring, for 3 minutes until golden. Reduce the heat to medium, then add the onion, pepper, carrot and paprika and cook for a further 2 minutes.

2   Add the rice and thyme sprigs, then stir in the chopped tomatoes and stock and season well. Simmer for 15-20 minutes, stirring occasionally, until the rice is cooked through.

3   Scatter over the parsley and serve with the lemon halves on the side for squeezing over.

The paella can be frozen in an airtight container for up to 3 months.

8   **SmartPoints value per serving**

One-pot wonder

'Here's another crowd-pleaser, perfect for feeding the hordes, as I frequently have to do! I haven't found anyone yet who doesn't love it.' **SUE**

Asian-style tuna steaks

serves 4   prep time 10 minutes + marinating   cook time 8 minutes

Tuna is a great alternative to classic beef steak – it's just as meaty, but as it's a ZeroPoint food, you can use your SmartPoints on sides and extras.

3 tablespoons finely chopped fresh coriander

1 red chilli, deseeded and finely chopped, plus extra sliced red chilli, to serve

3cm piece fresh ginger, peeled and finely grated

2 garlic cloves, crushed

Grated zest and juice of 1 lime

1 tablespoon soy sauce

4 x 220g tuna steaks

Calorie controlled cooking spray

2 x 250g pouches microwave brown rice

Lime slices, to serve

1 In a large non-metallic bowl, combine 2 tablespoons of the coriander, the chilli, ginger, garlic, lime zest and juice and soy sauce. Add the tuna steaks, turning to coat, then cover with clingfilm and transfer to the fridge to marinate for 2 hours, or overnight.

2 Remove the tuna steaks from the fridge 30 minutes before cooking, transfer to a plate using a slotted spoon, and allow to come to room temperature. Discard the leftover marinade.

3 Set a nonstick griddle pan over a high heat and mist with cooking spray, then cook the tuna steaks for 3 minutes each side for medium or 5 minutes each side for well done.

4 Cook the rice to pack instructions. Serve the tuna steaks with the rice, with the remaining coriander and extra chilli scattered over, and the lime slices on the side.

 6 SmartPoints value per serving

Cook's tip

Try serving this with the Asian cucumber salad, p109, for an extra 1 SmartPoint per serving.

Summer sides

Brighten up mealtimes with these simple ideas – they're full of summer's best vegetables and flavours.

Roasted tomato & rocket salad
serves 4
prep time 10 minutes   **cook time 40 minutes**

Preheat the oven to 150°C, fan 130°C, gas mark 2. Put 2 quartered **vine tomatoes**, 4 halved **plum tomatoes** and 5 halved **cherry tomatoes** in a shallow roasting tin in a single layer. Sprinkle over 2 crushed **garlic cloves** and 1 teaspoon **dried tarragon**, then drizzle over 1 tablespoon **extra virgin olive oil** and ½ tablespoon **balsamic vinegar**. Season to taste. Roast for 40 minutes, basting the tomatoes halfway through, until tender. Put 60g **rocket** in a serving bowl, add the roasted tomatoes and any juices, then gently toss to combine. Serve warm or at room temperature.

    SmartPoints value per serving

Asian cucumber salad
serves 4
prep time 10 minutes + chilling   **cook time 2 minutes**

Bring 2 tablespoons **rice wine vinegar**, 2 teaspoons **caster sugar**, 1 teaspoon **sea salt** and 1 tablespoon finely chopped **fresh ginger** to a simmer in a small pan over a low heat. Gently cook until the sugar has dissolved, then set aside to cool. Put 1 thinly sliced **cucumber**, 6 trimmed and thinly sliced **radishes** and 2 tablespoons chopped **fresh mint** in a serving bowl and toss through the dressing. Let stand for 10 minutes, then serve.

    SmartPoints value per serving

Satay noodles
serves 4
prep time 5 minutes   **cook time 15 minutes**

Dissolve 24g **PBfit Original Powdered Nut Butter** in 60ml boiling water. Cook 4 x 60g **dried egg noodle** nests to pack instructions. Put a large nonstick pan or wok over a high heat and mist with **calorie controlled cooking spray**. Add a 3cm piece peeled and finely chopped **fresh ginger**, 1 crushed **garlic clove**, 2 trimmed and thinly sliced **spring onions** and 1 deseeded and chopped **red chilli** and cook, stirring, for 3 minutes until softened. Add the cooked noodles, peanut butter sauce, 1 tablespoon **soy sauce** and 1 tablespoon **fish sauce** and toss to combine. Squeeze over the juice of 1 **lime** and serve.

    SmartPoints value per serving

Summer sides

Jewelled giant couscous

serves 4
prep time 15 minutes   cook time 10 minutes

Put 200g **giant couscous** in a pan and cover with cold water, then bring to a boil over a medium heat. Cook for 6-8 minutes, until the grains are translucent and tender. Drain, refresh under cold running water, and drain again. In a serving bowl, combine the couscous, the grated zest and juice of 1 **lemon** and a small handful each of roughly chopped **fresh mint** and **fresh basil**. Season to taste. Add 70g chopped **dried apricots**, 100g **pomegranate seeds**, 1 deseeded and roughly chopped **yellow pepper** and 5 quartered **baby plum tomatoes** and gently fold to combine, then serve.

6   SmartPoints value per serving

2-ingredient flatbreads

serves 4   freezable
prep time 10 minutes   cook time 12 minutes

Combine 100g **self-raising flour** and 100g **fat-free natural yogurt** in a bowl until the mixture comes together. Turn the dough out onto a lightly floured work surface, gently knead for a couple of minutes, then divide into 4 even pieces. Roll out to a thickness of 5mm. Put a large, dry, nonstick frying pan over a high heat. Add the flatbreads and cook for 2-3 minutes each side until lightly golden and puffed up; you'll need to do this in batches. The flatbreads can be frozen tightly wrapped in clingfilm for up to 3 months.

3   SmartPoints value per flatbread

10-minute coleslaw

serves 4
prep time 10 minutes   cook time 12 minutes

In a serving bowl, combine ⅓ finely sliced **white cabbage**, 1 coarsely grated **carrot**, 2 trimmed and thinly sliced **spring onions**, 1 small crushed **garlic clove**, 2 tablespoons **Alpro Simply Plain yogurt alternative**, 1 tablespoon vegan **wholegrain mustard** and the grated zest and juice of ½ **lemon**, then serve.

0   SmartPoints value per serving

Summer snacks & desserts

Treat yourself to this season's best fruits and savoury flavours with these easy ideas.

Summer pudding

serves 6
prep time 15 minutes + chilling
cook time 10 minutes

Put 100g **golden caster sugar** and 75ml water in a large pan set over a low heat. Cook until the sugar has dissolved, then increase the heat and gently boil for 3-4 minutes until syrupy. Remove from the heat and add 350g **raspberries**, 350g **blackberries** and 350g hulled and quartered **strawberries**, then set aside to cool. Trim the crusts from 8 slices **white bread**. Using a small round cutter, cut a circle from 1 of the trimmed slices to fit the bottom of a 1.2-litre pudding basin lined with clingfilm. Line the sides of the basin with 5 of the bread slices, overlapping the layers so there are no gaps. Drain the fruit, reserving the syrup, and add to the basin. Spoon over 2 tablespoons of the reserved syrup. Cover the fruit with the remaining bread, then cover with the edges of the clingfilm. Put a saucer on top of the basin and put a heavy object on top, such as tinned food. Transfer the basin to a shallow dish and chill for 6 hours, or overnight. Turn the pudding out onto a serving plate and brush any white areas with syrup, then top with 150g **mixed berries**. Serve with the remaining syrup and 150g **0% fat natural Greek yogurt**.

6 SmartPoints value per serving

Summer snacks & desserts

Griddled watermelon

serves 4
prep time 5 minutes
cook time 5 minutes

Combine 300g **0% fat natural Greek yogurt**, the grated zest and juice of 1 **lime** plus 1 tablespoon **lime juice**, ½ tablespoon chopped **fresh mint** and 1 tablespoon **clear honey** in a mixing bowl. Cover with clingfilm and chill until needed. Cut a 1.2kg **watermelon** into 12 wedges, leaving the rind on. Set a griddle pan over a high heat. Add the watermelon and griddle for 30 seconds each side until lightly charred; you'll need to do this in batches. Serve the watermelon with the yogurt sauce on the side for dipping and extra **fresh mint leaves** scattered over the top.

1   SmartPoints value per serving

Griddled spring onion dip

serves 6
prep time 20 minutes   cook time 10 minutes

Preheat the oven to 200°C, fan 180°C, gas mark 6. Mist 4 **WW White Wraps** with **calorie controlled cooking spray**, then cut into triangles. Arrange in single layers on two baking trays lined with baking paper, then bake for 7-8 minutes or until golden. Season to taste, then set aside to cool. Meanwhile, mist 8 trimmed **spring onions** with cooking spray. Put a griddle pan over a medium-high heat and griddle the spring onions for 6-7 minutes, turning, until tender. Remove from the pan, then roughly chop and set aside to cool. Put the spring onions in a food processor with 1 crushed **garlic clove** and the juice of ½ **lemon** and blitz until smooth. Stir the spring onion mixture through 300g **0% fat natural Greek yogurt**, sprinkle over **freshly ground black pepper** and the grated zest of ½ **lemon** and serve with the tortilla chips.

2   SmartPoints value per serving

Strawberry sundaes

serves 4   prep time 15 minutes

Put 150g hulled **strawberries** and 1 tablespoon **caster sugar** in a food processor and blitz to a smooth purée. Push through a fine sieve and discard any pips. Reserve 6 tablespoons of the purée, then swirl the remaining purée through 400g **0% fat natural Greek yogurt**. Divide the yogurt and strawberry swirl between 4 sundae glasses and layer with 40g crushed **meringue nests** and 250g hulled and quartered **strawberries**. Top each glass with 1 scoop **low-fat vanilla ice cream**, then drizzle over the reserved strawberry purée to serve.

7   SmartPoints value per serving

Banana & peanut butter 'ice cream'

serves 4
prep time 10 minutes + freezing

Cut 4 **bananas** into 3cm chunks and spread out on a baking tray. Freeze for 2-3 hours, or until solid. Put the frozen bananas and 100ml **skimmed milk** in a food processor and blitz until smooth. Add 2 tablespoons **smooth peanut butter** and ½ teaspoon **ground cinnamon**, then blitz again until combined. Transfer to a freezer-proof container and freeze for 1 hour, then serve with extra sliced **bananas**.

3   SmartPoints value per serving

Autumn

Bonfire

Night is on the horizon and evenings are drawing in – autumn is all about cooler weather, comforting meals and getting back into your routine after a fun-filled summer. But don't let busier days and longer nights put you off! Autumn's filled with delicious ZeroPoint veg, like squash, pumpkin and sweet potato, all of which work brilliantly in one-pot dishes like chilli and curry. And because these all-in-one meals are easy to batch-cook at the weekend, you'll always have a healthy dinner to hand.

'Warming soups are great on those chilly autumnal evenings, making them perfect for Bonfire Night.'

TONY

Autumn breakfasts

Get back into your routine with easy, fuss-free brekkies, from warming porridge to a simple, delicious omelette.

Rainbow veggie slice

serves 4   prep time 10 minutes   cook time 25 minutes

Preheat the oven to 180°C, fan 160°C, gas mark 4. Put 200g **young leaf spinach** in a microwave-safe bowl, cover and cook on high for 2 minutes or until wilted. Cool slightly, then squeeze out any excess liquid and roughly chop. Put the spinach in a large bowl and add 1 large peeled and grated **carrot**, 1 large grated **courgette**, 1 deseeded and sliced **red pepper** and 1 thinly sliced **red onion**. In a separate bowl, lightly beat 7 large **eggs**, then add to the veg mixture along with 3 crushed **garlic cloves** and 55g **plain flour**. Season well and stir to combine. Mist a 23cm x 33cm baking dish with **calorie controlled cooking spray**, then add the veg and egg mixture. Bake for 20 minutes, or until the egg has set and the veg is cooked, then serve.

①   SmartPoints value per serving

Porridge with blueberry compote

serves 4
prep time 5 minutes
cook time 15 minutes

Put 300g frozen **blueberries** in a pan with 2 tablespoons water and ½ tablespoon **clear honey** and put over a medium-low heat. Cook for 4-5 minutes until heated through, crushing the berries slightly with a wooden spoon. Set aside. Put 120g **porridge oats** and 750ml **skimmed milk** in a large pan and bring to a boil. Reduce the heat to a simmer and cook for 4-5 minutes, stirring, until the porridge is thick. Roughly chop 10g **unsalted pistachio nuts**. Divide the porridge between 4 bowls and spoon over the compote. Top each bowl with 1 tablespoon **0% fat natural Greek yogurt**, with the pistachio nuts scattered over to serve.

⑦   SmartPoints value per serving

Sweet potato & chorizo hash

serves 4
prep time 15 minutes
cook time 30 minutes

Put a large, lidded nonstick pan over a medium heat and add 120g cubed **cooking chorizo**. Cook for 3-4 minutes, or until its oils are released, then transfer to a small bowl. Put 2 thinly sliced **red onions** in the pan and cook for 3-4 minutes, then add a 300g pack **prepared butternut squash and sweet potato** and ½ teaspoon **smoked paprika**. Cook for another 5 minutes. Cover, then continue to cook for 10 minutes, until the veg is soft. Add 250g halved **cherry tomatoes** and 200g **young leaf spinach**, then cover and cook for another 5 minutes, until the spinach has wilted and the tomatoes are soft. Bring a large pan of water to a boil and add 1 tablespoon **white wine vinegar**. Crack 1 **egg** into a ramekin. Stir the water to create a whirlpool and gently slide in the egg. Cook for 2-3 minutes, then transfer to a plate lined with kitchen paper. Repeat with 3 more **eggs**. Stir the chorizo into the hash, then serve topped with the eggs, a small handful of chopped **fresh flat-leaf parsley**, and **freshly ground black pepper**.

Mushroom & tomato omelette

serves 1
prep time 5 minutes   cook time 15 minutes

Mist a nonstick frying pan with **calorie controlled cooking spray** and put over a medium-high heat. Add 100g halved **button mushrooms** and cook for 4-5 minutes until golden, then add 100g halved **cherry tomatoes** and 2 chopped **garlic cloves**. Cook for 1-2 minutes, then stir through 1 tablespoon roughly chopped **fresh basil** and season to taste. Transfer the mixture to a bowl, cover and keep warm. Wipe the pan clean. In a small bowl, combine 3 **eggs** and 1 tablespoon roughly chopped **fresh basil**, then season to taste. Mist the pan again and put over a medium heat. Pour in the egg mixture and tilt the pan so the base is covered. Allow the eggs to set, then push the cooked edges into the centre using a spatula, letting any uncooked egg run into the gaps. Repeat until the centre is almost fully set. Fold the omelette in half, then spoon over the veg mixture and scatter over some extra **fresh basil** to serve.

0 SmartPoints value per serving

5 SmartPoints value per serving

Spanish-style mussels

serves 4   prep time 5 minutes   cook time 40 minutes

Fresh mussels come into season around October – so why not start the season with this tasty recipe using a tomato sauce flavoured with paprika, garlic and chorizo?

1.5kg mussels

50g cooking chorizo, cubed

2 shallots, finely chopped

1 garlic clove, crushed

1 tablespoon smoked paprika

2 x 400g tins chopped tomatoes

200ml hot vegetable stock, made with ½ stock cube

2 tablespoons finely chopped fresh flat-leaf parsley

Lemon wedges, to serve

4 x 50g slices sourdough bread, to serve

1   Scrub the mussels clean, removing any beards and discarding mussels that are cracked or don't close when tapped gently on the work surface.

2   Put a large, lidded pan over a medium heat. Put the chorizo and shallots in the pan and cook for 7-8 minutes, until the chorizo is crisp and the shallots are tender. Add the garlic and paprika and cook for a further 1 minute.

3   Add the tomatoes and stock, reduce the heat and gently simmer the sauce, covered, for 25 minutes. Add the mussels and stir to combine. Cover and steam for 4-5 minutes, or until the mussels have opened; discard any that remain shut. Stir through the parsley, then serve with the lemon wedges and bread on the side.

5   **SmartPoints value per serving**

Cook's tip
Serve this with the Orzo pasta with pesto dressing, p157, for an extra 6 SmartPoints per serving.

Bean & butternut squash chilli

serves 4   freezable   prep time 10 minutes   cook time 55 minutes

Warm up on cooler evenings with this tasty one-pot dish. ZeroPoint beans and butternut squash help to keep it low in SmartPoints, while ground spices add plenty of flavour.

Calorie controlled cooking spray

1 large onion, finely chopped

2 garlic cloves, crushed

½ tablespoon ground cumin

½ tablespoon ground coriander

1 tablespoon smoked paprika, plus extra to serve

1 teaspoon onion granules

1 tablespoon chipotle paste

Large handful fresh coriander, stalks and leaves separated and chopped

600g prepared butternut squash, cubed

500ml vegetable stock, made with 1 stock cube

400g tin chopped tomatoes

2 x 400g tins red kidney beans, drained and rinsed

100g fat-free natural yogurt, to serve

1. Mist a large, lidded, nonstick pan with cooking spray and cook the onion for 6-8 minutes over a medium heat until soft. Add the garlic, cumin, ground coriander, smoked paprika and onion granules and cook for another 1 minute, stirring constantly.

2. Add the chipotle paste, coriander stalks and butternut squash and cook for another 2 minutes, then add the stock and chopped tomatoes. Season to taste, then cover and gently simmer for 30 minutes. Add the beans and cook, uncovered, for another 15 minutes. Stir through most of the coriander leaves.

3. Serve the chilli topped with the yogurt, with the remaining coriander leaves scattered over and a sprinkling of smoked paprika.

The chilli can be frozen in an airtight container for up to 2 months.

1 SmartPoints value per serving

Cook's tip
Serve this with the Oven-baked quinoa, p154, for an extra 6 SmartPoints per serving.

Aubergine & tomato curry

serves 4 **freezable** **prep time 15 minutes** **cook time 50 minutes**

This simple veg curry is bursting with flavour, thanks to a variety of spices, curry leaves and bright, fresh coriander.

Calorie controlled cooking spray

1 large onion, finely sliced

2cm piece fresh ginger, peeled and finely grated

3 garlic cloves, crushed

1 tablespoon mild curry powder

1 teaspoon ground coriander

1 teaspoon ground cumin

2 tablespoons tomato purée

2 aubergines, trimmed and cubed

8 dried curry leaves

500g large tomatoes, roughly chopped

400g tin chopped tomatoes

500ml hot vegetable stock, made with 1 stock cube

Grated zest and juice of 1 lime, plus wedges to serve

2 tablespoons finely chopped fresh coriander, plus extra, to serve

1 Mist a large, lidded pan with cooking spray and put over a medium-high heat. Cook the onion for 6-8 minutes until soft, then add the ginger, garlic and spices and cook for another 2 minutes.

2 Stir in the tomato purée and aubergines and cook for a further 3-4 minutes. Add the curry leaves, all of the tomatoes and the stock, reduce the heat and gently simmer, covered, for 25 minutes, then remove the lid and continue to cook for 10 minutes. Remove and discard the curry leaves, then stir through the lime zest and juice and the coriander.

3 Sprinkle over the extra fresh coriander, then serve the curry with the lime wedges on the side.

The curry can be frozen in an airtight container for up to 2 months.

 SmartPoints value per serving

Full of flavour

'This is typical of the kind of warming, flavoursome recipe I love. It includes aubergines, ginger, coriander and lime – some of my favourite ingredients. Serve it with the Spicy turmeric rice, p154, for an extra 6 SmartPoints per serving.'
ELISHA

Steak & caramelised onion sandwiches

serves 4   **prep time 20 minutes**   **cook time 25 minutes**

A classic steak and onion sarnie gets an upgrade with a deliciously creamy, zesty spread made using mayonnaise, lemon and horseradish sauce.

Calorie controlled cooking spray

1 large onion, finely sliced

4 x 90g thin-cut lean beef steaks

4 tablespoons reduced-fat mayonnaise

Grated zest of ½ lemon, plus 2 teaspoons lemon juice

½ tablespoon horseradish sauce

8 x 50g slices sourdough bread

30g rocket

1 Mist a large, nonstick, heavy-based frying pan with cooking spray and cook the onion over a medium-low heat for 20-25 minutes, stirring regularly, until golden brown. Transfer to a plate and set aside.

2 Mist the pan with more cooking spray and increase the heat to high. Season the steaks, then fry for 1 minute each side. Transfer to a plate and set aside to rest for 2 minutes, then slice into strips.

3 In a small bowl, combine the mayonnaise, lemon zest and juice and the horseradish sauce. Toast the bread, then spread ½ tablespoon of the mayonnaise mixture over each slice. Top 4 slices of toast with the rocket, steak and onions, then top with the remaining toast slices. Serve immediately.

(10)   **SmartPoints value per serving**

Cook's tip
Serve this with the Butternut squash wedges, p157, for an extra 1 SmartPoint per serving.

Lentil Bolognese

serves 4   freezable   prep time 15 minutes   cook time 1 hour 10 minutes

This vegan take on a family favourite meal tastes just as delicious as the original, and uses filling lentils as a base for the Bolognese sauce.

Calorie controlled cooking spray

1 onion, finely chopped

2 carrots, finely chopped

1 celery stick, finely chopped

2 garlic cloves, crushed

2 tablespoons tomato purée

300g dried red lentils

400g tin chopped tomatoes

900ml vegetable stock, made with 2 stock cubes

1 tablespoon Marmite yeast extract

5 sprigs fresh thyme

3 sprigs fresh rosemary

2 bay leaves

300g spaghetti

2 tablespoons grated vegan hard cheese alternative, to serve

1 Mist a large, lidded, nonstick frying pan with cooking spray and set over a medium heat. Add the onion, carrots and celery and cook for 8-10 minutes until soft, then add the garlic and tomato purée and cook for another 1 minute.

2 Stir in the lentils, chopped tomatoes, stock, Marmite, thyme, rosemary and bay leaves and simmer for about 1 hour, covered, until the sauce has thickened and the lentils are tender. Remove and discard the thyme, rosemary and bay leaves.

3 Meanwhile, cook the spaghetti to pack instructions, then drain. Toss the pasta and sauce together and serve with the cheese alternative scattered over the top.

The sauce can be frozen in an airtight container for up to 3 months.

9   **SmartPoints value per serving**

Great for freezing

'Lentil Bolognese is a great and inexpensive dish for a busy mum. You can make a big batch, portion it up and freeze it. Hey presto, dinner's ready.' **SELEN**

Mushroom & leek tagliatelle

serves 4   **prep time 10 minutes**   **cook time 10 minutes**

Smooth and creamy, this moreish pasta tastes indulgent, but thanks to half-fat crème fraîche, the delectable sauce won't derail your Daily SmartPoints Budget.

260g tagliatelle

Calorie controlled cooking spray

1 large leek, trimmed and thinly sliced

250g chestnut mushrooms, sliced

2 garlic cloves, crushed

150g half-fat crème fraîche

Grated zest of 1 lemon, plus lemon wedges, to serve

2 tablespoons finely chopped fresh flat-leaf parsley, plus extra, to serve

2 tablespoons finely grated vegetarian Italian-style hard cheese

1 Cook the pasta to pack instructions and drain, reserving about 200ml of the cooking water.

2 Meanwhile, mist a nonstick pan with cooking spray and put over a medium heat. Add the leek and cook for 3-4 minutes until soft, then add the mushrooms and cook for another 5-6 minutes, until tender. Add the garlic and cook for another 1 minute.

3 Stir in the crème fraîche, lemon zest and parsley, then add a little of the reserved cooking water to loosen the sauce. Toss together the pasta and sauce, then serve with the cheese and extra parsley scattered over, with the lemon wedges on the side.

10   **SmartPoints value per serving**

Cook's tip

Try swapping the leek for 100g young leaf spinach – add it at the end with the pasta and let it wilt into the sauce. The SmartPoints will be the same.

Spinach & mushroom galette

serves 4   prep time 20 minutes + chilling   cook time 1 hour minutes

A galette is a rustic, fuss-free tart – and this savoury version uses a combination of shallots, mushrooms and spinach, as well as melting mozzarella, as a tasty filling.

80g wholemeal flour

120g plain flour

¼ teaspoon salt

1 tablespoon dried thyme

100g low-fat spread

1 egg, lightly beaten, plus 1 egg yolk

500g young leaf spinach

Calorie controlled cooking spray

2 shallots, finely sliced

250g chestnut mushrooms, sliced

2 garlic cloves, crushed

Small pinch nutmeg

100g light mozzarella, torn

Salad leaves, to serve

1   Put the flours, salt and ½ tablespoon of the thyme in a food processor, then add the spread by spoonfuls. Blitz the mixture until it resembles breadcrumbs. Add the beaten egg and blitz until a dough forms. Form the dough into a disc, wrap in clingfilm and put in the fridge to chill for 30 minutes.

2   Put the spinach in a large colander, then pour over a large kettle of boiling water until wilted. Squeeze out any excess water using the back of a spoon, then roughly chop and set aside.

3   Mist a nonstick pan with cooking spray and put over a medium heat. Add the shallots and cook for 7-8 minutes until soft, then add the mushrooms and cook for another 5-6 minutes, until tender. Add the garlic and nutmeg and cook for another 1 minute, then remove from the heat and stir in the spinach. Season well, then set aside to cool for 5 minutes. Stir in the mozzarella. Preheat the oven to 200°C, fan 180°C, gas mark 6 and line a baking tray with baking paper.

4   Roll the pastry out into a rough 40cm diameter circle (it should be about 3mm thick) and transfer to the prepared baking tray. Spread the mushroom and spinach mixture over the pastry, leaving a 5cm border. Bring the edges up and over the filling. Put the egg yolk in a small bowl, then lightly beat with a fork and brush it over the exposed pastry. Bake for 40-45 minutes until golden and crisp. Serve the galette with the salad leaves on the side.

Cook's tip
Serve this with the Garlic & chilli roasted cauliflower, p157, for an extra 1 SmartPoint per serving.

 9   SmartPoints value per serving

Chicken casserole with dumplings

serves 4 freezable prep time 20 minutes cook time 1 hour

Hearty and wholesome, this flavourful stew is sure to warm up even the coolest evenings, and is great for feeding the whole family.

4 x 165g skinless chicken breast fillets, cut into large chunks

150g self-raising flour, plus 2 tablespoons

Calorie controlled cooking spray

1 onion, finely chopped

3 carrots, sliced into 5mm rounds

1 celery stick, thinly sliced

460g potatoes, roughly chopped

2 garlic cloves, crushed

½ tablesoon Dijon mustard

850ml chicken stock, made with 1 stock cube

2 sprigs fresh rosemary

2 sprigs fresh thyme

1 bay leaf

1 tablespoon cornflour

120g fat-free natural yogurt

2 tablespoons finely chopped fresh tarragon, plus extra, to serve

Steamed green beans, to serve

1 Put the chicken and 2 tablespoons of the flour in a large bowl, season to taste and toss together until the chicken is coated in the flour.

2 Mist a 2-litre flameproof, lidded, nonstick casserole dish with cooking spray and put over a medium heat. Add the onion, carrots, celery and potatoes and cook for 6-8 minutes until just soft, then add the garlic and mustard and cook for another 2 minutes.

3 Add the chicken and cook, stirring, for a further 2-3 minutes, then add the stock, rosemary, thyme and bay leaf. Cover and gently simmer for 20 minutes, then remove the lid. In a small bowl, combine the cornflour and a little of the liquid from the casserole to form a thin paste, then stir it back into the dish. Cook, uncovered, for 10 additional minutes.

4 Meanwhile, combine the remaining flour, the yogurt and tarragon in a small bowl until a dough forms, then divide into 8 and roll into balls. Put the dumplings on the surface of the stew, then cover and cook for 10-15 minutes, until the dumplings have puffed up and are cooked through. Serve the dumplings and stew with the extra tarragon scattered over, a sprinkling of freshly ground black pepper and the beans on the side.

The casserole can be frozen without the dumplings for up to 2 months. Defrost and bring to a simmer, then add the dumplings as in the recipe.

8 **SmartPoints value per serving**

Autumn cheer
'You want something warming when the days are getting colder, and this dish ticks all the boxes. My daughters love the dumplings!' **NADINE**

Cheesy vegetable bake

serves 4 **prep time 10 minutes** **cook time 40 minutes**

Cauliflower, broccoli, carrot, leek and an indulgent cheese sauce combine in this hearty bake. A fresh green salad on the side is the perfect partner.

1 cauliflower, cut into florets
1 broccoli, cut into florets
1 carrot, cut into ½cm rounds
1 leek, trimmed and finely sliced
2 tablespoons low-fat spread
2 garlic cloves, crushed
½ tablespoon wholegrain mustard
2 tablespoons plain flour
500ml skimmed milk
100g half-fat Cheddar cheese, coarsely grated
40g panko breadcrumbs
½ tablespoon olive oil
½ tablespoon snipped fresh chives
Green salad leaves
Juice of ½ lemon

1. Bring a large pan of water to a boil and cook the cauliflower, broccoli and carrot for 6 minutes, adding the leek for the final minute. Drain and set aside.

2. Preheat the oven to 190°C, fan 170°C, gas mark 5. Melt the spread in a large pan over a medium heat, then add the garlic and mustard. Stir in the flour and cook for 1 minute, then whisk in a little of the milk until smooth. Gradually whisk in the remaining milk, bring to a simmer and cook, stirring, for 2 minutes until the sauce is thick enough to coat the back of a spoon.

3. Add most of cheese, then season to taste and stir to melt. Remove from the heat, add the boiled vegetables and stir to combine.

4. Transfer the cheese and veg mixture to a 2.5-litre baking dish. In a small bowl, combine the breadcrumbs, olive oil and chives, then scatter over the veg. Sprinkle over the remaining cheese. Bake for 25 minutes until golden and bubbling. Toss the salad leaves and lemon juice together, then serve the veg bake with the salad on the side.

7 SmartPoints value per serving

Cook's tip
Try using other veg in this bake – pumpkin or butternut squash would also work well, and the SmartPoints would remain the same.

Chicken & broccoli soup

serves 4   freezable   prep time 10 minutes   cook time 40 minutes

This soup is perfect for packed lunches or meal planning – simply prep in advance and portion into freezer bags for a warming bowl in minutes.

1½ litres chicken stock, made with 3 stock cubes

2 x 165g skinless chicken breast fillets

400g potatoes, cut into chunks

Calorie controlled cooking spray

2 shallots, finely chopped

2 garlic cloves, crushed

1 broccoli, cut into small florets

2 teaspoons ground white pepper

70g fat-free natural yogurt, plus extra to serve

1 tablespoon snipped fresh chives, to serve

1 Put the stock in a large, lidded pan and bring to a simmer. Add the chicken and potatoes, cover and continue to simmer for 20 minutes, or until the chicken is cooked through. Using a slotted spoon, transfer the chicken to a plate and roughly shred using two forks.

2 Mist a large, heavy-bottomed nonstick pan with cooking spray and fry the shallots for 6-8 minutes over a medium heat until soft. Add the garlic and cook for another 1 minute. Add the broccoli and cook for a further 2 minutes, then add a ladleful of the stock to the pan and use a wooden spoon to scrape up any browned bits. Put the broccoli mixture in the pan with the stock and potatoes. Add the white pepper, then stir and simmer for 7-8 minutes until the broccoli is tender. Blitz using a stick blender until smooth. Season to taste, then stir in the yogurt and chicken.

3 Serve with the extra yogurt spooned over and the chives sprinkled over the top.

The soup can be frozen in an airtight container for up to 3 months.

3 **SmartPoints value per serving**

Quick & easy
'Soups are a brilliant way of making a quick meal, and extra portions can be frozen as healthy ready-meals that can be reheated in minutes. Serve this with a 65g brown roll for an extra 5 SmartPoints per serving.' **TONY**

Fish pie with herby cauliflower mash

serves 4**prep time 15 minutes****cook time 40 minutes**

Who doesn't enjoy a fish pie? It's a classic dish that's loved by all, and it's made even better by a flavourful, low in SmartPoints cauliflower mash topping.

1 large cauliflower, cut into florets

150g half-fat Cheddar cheese, coarsely grated

1 tablespoon snipped fresh chives

2 tablespoons finely chopped fresh flat-leaf parsley

500ml skimmed milk

450g fish pie mix

30g low-fat spread

1 garlic clove, crushed

2 teaspoons Dijon mustard

25g plain flour

180g raw peeled prawns

100g frozen peas

Steamed Tenderstem broccoli, to serve

1 Cook the cauliflower in a pan of boiling water for 8 minutes, then drain and mash until smooth. Season well, then stir in 30g of the cheese and half of the herbs and set aside. Preheat the oven to 190°C, fan 170°C, gas mark 5.

2 Put the milk and fish pie mix in a large pan, bring to a gentle simmer and cook for 4 minutes. Transfer the fish to a plate using a slotted spoon, and reserve the milk.

3 Melt the spread in the pan over a medium heat and stir in the garlic and mustard. Add the flour and cook for 2 minutes. Gradually whisk in the reserved milk, bring to a simmer and cook for 2 minutes until the sauce is thick enough to coat the back of a spoon. Season to taste. Add 90g of the cheese, the fish pie mix, the prawns, peas and the remaining herbs. Cook, stirring, for 1 minute, then pour the mixture into a 2.5-litre baking dish and top with the cauliflower mash. Sprinkle over the remaining cheese and bake for 25 minutes, until golden and bubbling. Serve with the broccoli on the side.

6 SmartPoints value per serving

Italian-style crumbed turkey

serves 4   **prep time 20 minutes**   **cook time 1 hour 10 minutes**

Tender turkey breast steaks are coated in panko breadcrumbs and topped with
a delicious light mozzarella and herby passata sauce.

Calorie controlled cooking spray

1 small onion, finely chopped

2 garlic cloves, crushed

500g passata

2 tablespoons finely chopped fresh basil, plus extra, to serve

4 tablespoons plain flour

2 eggs, lightly beaten

70g panko breadcrumbs

4 x 115g skinless turkey breast steaks

125g light mozzarella, sliced

Green salad, to serve

1   Mist a small nonstick pan with cooking spray, add the onion and cook over a medium heat for 6-8 minutes until soft. Add the garlic and cook for another 1 minute, then add the passata and gently simmer for 25 minutes. Season to taste, then stir in the basil. Preheat the oven to 200°C, fan 180°C, gas mark 6.

2   Put the flour, eggs and breadcrumbs on 3 separate plates, then dip each turkey steak in the flour, the egg, and finally, the breadcrumbs. Set aside.

3   Mist a large nonstick pan with cooking spray and put over a medium heat. Cook the turkey for 3 minutes on each side, then transfer to a baking tray and bake for 10 minutes. Spoon the sauce over the centre of the turkey, then top with the mozzarella slices and bake for a further 20 minutes. Serve with the extra basil scattered over and the salad on the side.

6   **SmartPoints value per serving**

Cook's tip
Serve this with the Butternut squash wedges, p157, for an extra 1 SmartPoint per serving.

Harissa sausage traybake

serves 4   prep time 15 minutes   cook time 45 minutes

Super simple and quick to pull together, this tasty traybake makes the perfect all-in-one supper for those busy weeknights.

620g new potatoes, quartered

200g mixed cherry tomatoes, halved

2 red onions, cut into wedges

4 garlic cloves, unpeeled

8 reduced-fat Cumberland sausages

2 tablespoons harissa paste

½ tablespoon olive oil

1 red and 1 yellow pepper, both deseeded and roughly chopped

2 tablespoons roughly chopped fresh coriander, to serve

Lemon wedges, to serve

1   Preheat the oven to 200°C, fan 180°C, gas mark 6. Put the potatoes, tomatoes, onions, garlic, sausages, harissa paste, olive oil and peppers in a large roasting tin and toss to combine. Season to taste and bake for 35-40 minutes, stirring halfway through, until the potatoes are golden and tender and the sausages are cooked through.

2   Serve with the coriander scattered over and with the lemon wedges on the side.

7   **SmartPoints value per serving**

Cook's tip
Serve this with the Mixed bean salad, p154, for an extra 1 SmartPoint per serving.

Chicken & bacon risotto

serves 4   **prep time 10 minutes**   **cook time 45 minutes**

Comforting risotto gets a flavour upgrade thanks to smoky bacon, moist chicken and fresh herbs – perfect for entertaining.

Calorie controlled cooking spray

8 smoked bacon medallions, roughly chopped

2 shallots, thinly sliced

2 garlic cloves, crushed

300g Arborio risotto rice

1 litre hot chicken stock, made with 1 stock cube

3 tablespoons finely grated Parmesan

2 tablespoons finely chopped fresh flat-leaf parsley

2 x 165g cooked skinless chicken breast fillets, shredded

1 Mist a large nonstick pan with cooking spray and put over a medium heat. Add the bacon and cook for 4-5 minutes, stirring, until golden, then transfer to a plate. Mist the pan with additional cooking spray and cook the shallots for 6-8 minutes. Add the garlic and cook for another 1 minute.

2 Stir in the rice and cook for 2 minutes, then add the stock a ladleful at a time, adding a final ladleful after all the liquid has been absorbed. This should take about 25-30 minutes.

3 Stir in most of the Parmesan and parsley, along with the bacon and chicken. Season to taste and serve with the remaining Parmesan and parsley scattered over.

10 **SmartPoints value per serving**

Chicken winner
'I'm a fan of anything that's quick and easy to prepare – and this risotto really is faff-free. It uses ready-cooked chicken for maximum simplicity.' **JONNY**

Spicy beef mince with rosti topping

serves 4   prep time 25 minutes   cook time 1 hour 15 minutes

A blend of storecupboard seasonings, including cumin, coriander and smoked paprika help to keep this dish extra flavourful.

Calorie controlled cooking spray

1 onion, thinly sliced

3 carrots, 1 finely chopped and 2 grated

2 garlic cloves, crushed

½ tablespoon ground cumin

½ tablespoon ground coriander

2 teaspoons smoked paprika

2 teaspoons mild chilli powder

2 tablespoons tomato purée

400g extra lean 5% fat beef mince

2 x 400g tins chopped tomatoes

200g frozen peas

2 tablespoons finely chopped fresh coriander

200g potatoes, peeled and coarsely grated

2 parsnips, peeled and coarsely grated

1 tablespoon olive oil

Steamed sugar snap peas, to serve

1 Mist a large, flameproof, nonstick casserole dish with cooking spray and put over a medium heat. Add the onion and chopped carrot and cook for 10 minutes until just soft, then add the garlic, cumin, ground coriander, smoked paprika and chilli powder, and cook for another 1 minute.

2 Stir in the tomato purée and cook for another 1 minute, then add the mince. Cook for 5 minutes until brown, then add the chopped tomatoes. Season to taste and gently simmer for 15 minutes, stirring occasionally. Stir in the peas and fresh coriander.

3 Preheat the oven to 200°C, fan 180°C, gas mark 6. Put the mince mixture into a 2.5-litre baking dish. Put the grated potatoes in a clean kitchen towel and squeeze out as much water as possible, then put in a mixing bowl with the grated carrots and parsnips. Add the olive oil and toss to combine, then season to taste. Top the mince mixture with the grated veg mixture and bake for 35 minutes, until golden and crisp. Serve with the sugar snap peas on the side.

7   SmartPoints value per serving

Cook's tip
It's important to squeeze as much water as you can from the potatoes to help the topping become crisp when cooked.

Autumn sides

Make traybakes, casseroles and soups go further with these easy side dishes – some can even double up as a speedy meal!

Mixed bean salad

serves 4   **prep time 10 minutes**

Drain and rinse a 400g tin **mixed bean salad** in water, then put in a serving bowl with 1 tablespoon drained **capers** in brine, 2 trimmed and finely chopped **spring onions**, ¼ trimmed and finely chopped **cucumber**, ½ deseeded and finely chopped **red pepper**, a small handful of finely chopped **fresh mint**, the grated zest and juice of ½ **lemon** and 1 tablespoon **extra virgin olive oil**. Stir to combine, then serve.

1   SmartPoints value per serving

Oven-baked quinoa

serves 4
prep time 15 minutes   **cook time 20 minutes**

Preheat the oven to 200°C, fan 180°C, gas mark 6. Cook 200g **quinoa** to pack instructions, then drain and set aside. Set a large nonstick pan over a medium heat, mist with **calorie controlled cooking spray**, then add 1 finely chopped **onion** and cook for 6-8 minutes until soft. Add 1 crushed **garlic clove** and cook for another 1 minute, then add 1 chopped **courgette** and 30g trimmed and torn **kale** and cook for a further 5 minutes, stirring occasionally. Put the quinoa and veg in a large bowl, then add 2 cooked and chopped **beetroot**, 20g finely chopped **walnuts** and 1 tablespoon **red wine vinegar** and stir to combine. Transfer to a baking dish and scatter over 40g grated **half-fat Cheddar cheese**. Bake for 15-20 minutes until golden, then serve.

6   SmartPoints value per serving

Spicy turmeric rice

serves 4
prep time 5 minutes + standing   **cook time 10 minutes**

Put a large, lidded nonstick pan over a high heat and mist with **calorie controlled cooking spray**. Add 1 teaspoon **mustard seeds**, 6 **cardamom pods**, a 2cm piece peeled and thinly sliced **fresh ginger**, 1 deseeded and sliced **green chilli** and 5 **dried curry leaves**, and cook for 1 minute. Add 220g white **basmati rice** and ½ teaspoon **ground turmeric**, stir to combine and cook for an additional 2 minutes. Stir in 600ml **vegetable stock**, made with 1 stock cube. Cover and bring to a boil, then reduce the heat and simmer for 5 minutes. Remove from the heat and set aside, covered, for 25 minutes. Fluff the rice using a fork, then serve.

6   SmartPoints value per serving

Autumn sides

Butternut squash wedges
serves 4   **prep time 15 minutes**   **cook time 50 minutes**

Preheat the oven to 200°C, fan 180°C, gas mark 6. Cut 1 peeled and deseeded **butternut squash** into wedges and put in a large roasting tin with 1 crushed **garlic clove**, 2 teaspoons **dried sage** and 1 teaspoon **chilli flakes**. Mist with **calorie controlled cooking spray** and toss to combine. Roast for 35-40 minutes until tender and golden. Remove from the oven, sprinkle over 30g grated **vegetarian Italian-style hard cheese**. Return to the oven for a further 8 minutes, then serve.

1   SmartPoints value per serving

Garlic & chilli roasted cauliflower
serves 4   **prep time 10 minutes**   **cook time 30 minutes**

Preheat the oven to 200°C, fan 180°C, gas mark 6. Cut 1 **cauliflower** into florets and put in a roasting tin with 3 sliced **garlic cloves**, ½ teaspoon **chilli flakes** and 1 teaspoon **dried thyme**, then mist with **calorie controlled cooking spray**. Season to taste. Roast for 25 minutes, tossing halfway through, until the cauliflower is tender and golden. Sprinkle over 30g grated **vegetarian Italian-style hard cheese** and return to the oven for a further 5 minutes. Sprinkle with 1 tablespoon chopped **fresh flat-leaf parsley** and **freshly ground black pepper** to serve.

1   SmartPoints value per serving

Orzo pasta with pesto dressing
serves 4   **prep time 10 minutes**   **cook time 10 minutes**

Cook 200g **orzo pasta** in a pan of boiling water to pack instructions. Put a small handful **fresh basil**, 15g **rocket**, 5g toasted **pine nuts**, 15g grated **vegetarian Italian-style hard cheese**, and the grated zest and juice of ½ **lemon** in a mini food processor with 3 tablespoons water. Blitz until smooth and season to taste. Toss the pesto dressing through the orzo pasta, then stir through 3 quartered **plum tomatoes**, 15g **rocket** and 5g toasted **pine nuts** to serve.

6   SmartPoints value per serving

Autumn snacks & desserts

Spend cosy nights in tucked up with these delicious snacks and tempting desserts, from spicy and savoury to indulgently sweet.

Plum crumble tart

serves 8
prep time 20 minutes   cook time 45 minutes

Preheat the oven to 180°C, fan 160°C, gas mark 4. Grease a 20cm-round fluted loose-bottomed tart tin with 1 teaspoon **low-fat spread**. Put 50g **walnuts** on a baking tray and roast for 5 minutes, until just golden. Set aside to cool slightly, then finely chop. Increase the oven temperature to 190°C, fan 170°C, gas mark 5. Put 150g **plain flour**, 100g **low-fat spread**, 50g **Demerara sugar**, ½ teaspoon **baking powder**, 1 teaspoon **cinnamon** and the walnuts in a large bowl and rub together using your fingertips until the mixture resembles coarse breadcrumbs. Press three-quarters of the mixture into the base and up the sides of the prepared tin. Halve 400g ripe **plums**, stones removed, and roughly chop, then put them in a large bowl with 10g **Demerara sugar**, 15g **cornflour** and 1 tablespoon **orange juice** and stir to combine. Spoon the plum mixture over the pastry case and sprinkle over the remaining crumble mixture. Put the tin on a baking tray and bake for 40-45 minutes or until golden and bubbling. Set aside to cool for 30 minutes in the tin, then remove from the tin and sieve over 1 teaspoon **icing sugar**, then cut into 8 and serve with 1 tablespoon **fat-free natural yogurt** per slice. Any leftover tart will keep in the fridge for up to 3 days.

7 SmartPoints value per serving

Heavenly snacks

'Baked sweet potato crisps have been sent to us from snack heaven. So deliciously moreish.' **SELEN**

Baked sweet potato crisps

serves 4
prep time 10 minutes
cook time 20 minutes

Preheat the oven to 200°C, fan 180°C, gas mark 6 and line two large baking trays with baking paper. Slice 400g **sweet potatoes** into 2mm thick rounds and put in a large bowl. Drizzle over 1 tablespoon **olive oil**, season to taste and toss to combine. Spread out the sweet potato crisps on the prepared baking trays in single layers. Bake for 18-20 minutes or until crisp. Allow to cool, then serve.

5 SmartPoints value per serving

Honey-roasted figs with ginger snap crumble

serves 6
prep time 5 minutes   cook time 20 minutes

Preheat the oven to 180°C, fan 160°C, gas mark 5. Line a shallow roasting tin with baking paper and add 12 halved **figs**. Spoon over 2 teaspoons **low-fat spread**. In a small bowl, combine the juice of 1 **orange** and 1 tablespoon **clear honey**, then pour over the figs. Bake for 20 minutes, until sticky and soft. Meanwhile, melt 1 teaspoon **low-fat spread** in a small pan over a low heat. Put 30g **reduced-fat ginger snaps** in a food bag and roughly crush using a rolling pin. Add the crushed ginger snaps to the pan with the spread, stir to combine, then transfer to a plate and chill until ready to serve. Divide the figs and 120g **half-fat crème fraîche** between 6 plates or bowls, then serve with the ginger snap crumbs sprinkled over.

4 SmartPoints value per serving

Blackberry mousse

serves 4
prep time 10 minutes

Put 375g defrosted **frozen blackberries** in a food processor. Blitz to a rough purée, then add 2 tablespoons **clear honey** and blitz again to combine. Pour the purée through a sieve and discard any pips, then return to the food processor. Add 1 large **egg white** and blitz until the mixture is light in colour and tripled in volume; this will take about 2-3 minutes. Spoon the mousse into 4 x 150ml glasses or ramekins. Scatter over 100g **fresh blackberries** and a small handful of **fresh mint leaves** to serve.

2 SmartPoints value per serving

Spicy popcorn

serves 4
prep time 5 minutes
cook time 10 minutes

Preheat the oven to 200°C, fan 180°C, gas mark 6. Put 1 tablespoon **sunflower oil** and 80g **popping corn** in a large, lidded pan and stir to combine. Cover and cook over a medium heat for 2-3 minutes, shaking often, until the corn starts to pop. Shake constantly until all the corn has popped, then remove from the heat and transfer to a large bowl, discarding any unpopped corn. In a small bowl, combine 1 teaspoon each **chilli flakes**, **hot paprika** and **freshly ground black pepper** and ¼ teaspoon **salt**. Sprinkle the mixture over the popcorn and stir to combine. Transfer the popcorn to a large baking tray and bake for 2 minutes, until crisp. Serve.

3 SmartPoints value per serving

Winter

Crackling fires, cosy afternoons in and, of course, Christmas –

winter may not bring the best weather, but there's still a lot to love about the chilly season. Chances are you'll be spending more time indoors, so you may have more time to cook from scratch – think slow-cooked stews and casseroles, nourishing soups, pies, pasta bakes, roast dinners and bowls of satisfying porridge for breakfast. Favourite winter flavours include warming spices like ginger and cinnamon, fragrant dried herbs, earthy root vegetables like beetroot and parsnips, and classic winter-time fruits like apples and pears.

'Christmas starts at the beginning of December for me. I always make a big batch of these gingerbread people and wrap them up for delicious gifts.'

ELLA

Winter breakfasts

Start your day off right with a warming, delicious brekkie. Whether you love a bowl of porridge or fancy something a bit more indulgent, there's plenty to choose from...

French toast with Black Forest compote
serves 4
prep time 5 minutes
cook time 25 minutes

Put 300g frozen **Black Forest fruits** in a pan with 2 tablespoons water and 1 tablespoon clear **honey**. Simmer for 3-4 minutes until the fruit is thawed. Remove from the heat and set aside. Break 2 large **eggs** into a shallow bowl. Add 50ml **skimmed milk**, 1 teaspoon **vanilla extract** and ½ teaspoon **ground cinnamon** and lightly beat with a fork. Mist a large pan with **calorie controlled cooking spray** and set over a medium heat. Dip 2 white **sandwich thins** into the egg mixture and allow to soak for a minute. Transfer the sandwich thins to the pan and cook for 2-3 minutes. Flip and cook for a further 2 minutes until golden. Repeat with 6 more sandwich thins, soaking one batch while another batch is cooking. Serve 2 sandwich thins per person, with the compote and 1 tablespoon **0% fat natural Greek yogurt** spooned over and **ground cinnamon** sprinkled over the top.

Coconut chia porridge
serves 4   prep time 5 minutes   cook time 5 minutes

Put 120g **porridge oats**, 350ml **skimmed milk** and 500ml water in a medium pan, bring to a simmer and cook over a medium heat for 4 minutes, stirring occasionally, until thickened. Stir in 50g **low-fat coconut yogurt**. Put the porridge in four bowls and top with another 80g **low-fat coconut yogurt**, 5g **chia seeds**, and the pulp and seeds of 2 **passion fruit**, divided between the bowls, then serve.

7 SmartPoints value per serving

7 SmartPoints value per serving

Veggie fry-up
serves 4
prep time 5 minutes
cook time 15 minutes

Mist a pan with **calorie controlled cooking spray** and put over a medium heat. Put 4 large **portobello mushrooms** and 4 halved **tomatoes** into the pan. and cook for 3 minutes. Turn, then cover and cook for a further 5 minutes. Season to taste, then transfer to an oven tray and keep warm. Cut 225g **light halloumi** into 8 slices, mist with cooking spray and sprinkle over ½ teaspoon **smoked paprika** and 1 teaspoon **dried oregano**. Mist the pan with more cooking spray and cook the halloumi for 2 minutes on each side. Transfer to the oven tray. Mist the pan again and crack in 4 **eggs**. Cook for 2-3 minutes or until the whites are set and the yolk is done to your liking. Meanwhile, pierce a 300g bag **young leaf spinach**, put on a microwave-safe plate and cook to pack instructions. Transfer to a bowl and press out any liquid using the back of a spoon. Toast 4 slices **WW Malted Danish Bread**, then spread 1 teaspoon **low-fat spread** on each slice. Divide the fried veg, halloumi and spinach between 4 plates, sprinkle over some **smoked paprika** and **dried oregano**, and serve with the toast.

Pesto shakshuka
serves 4   **prep time 5 minutes**   **cook time 35 minutes**

Mist a large, lidded nonstick frying pan with **calorie controlled cooking spray** and put over a medium heat. Add 1 thinly sliced **red onion** and 2 deseeded and sliced **red peppers** and cook for 6-8 minutes until soft, then add 1 crushed **garlic clove** and cook for another 1 minute. Add ½ tablespoon **balsamic vinegar** and 2 x 400g tins **chopped tomatoes**, season to taste and gently simmer for 15-20 minutes until slightly reduced. Stir in 2 tablespoons **reduced-fat green pesto** and 2 tablespoons torn **fresh basil leaves**, then reduce the heat to low. Make four hollows in the sauce with the back of a spoon, then crack in 4 **eggs** and cover the pan with the lid. Cook over a low heat for 6-7 minutes until the egg whites are set. Season with freshly ground black pepper and scatter over extra **fresh basil leaves**. Serve with 4 x 65g **crusty brown rolls**.

5 SmartPoints value per serving

7 SmartPoints value per serving

Winter mains

Beef & ale pie

serves 6   **freezable**   **prep time 15 minutes**   **cook time 2 hours 45 minutes**

What could be more perfect for a wintry evening than this slow-cooked beef, mushroom and dark ale stew, topped with golden puff pastry?

700g lean braising steak, cut into chunks

1½ tablespoons plain flour

Calorie controlled cooking spray

1 onion, thickly sliced

5 carrots, cut into 2cm chunks

250g chestnut mushrooms, quartered

120ml dark ale

600ml beef stock, made with 1 stock cube

1 bay leaf

3 sprigs fresh thyme

3 sprigs fresh rosemary

1½ teaspoons cornflour

2 teaspoons Marmite yeast extract

1 egg, lightly beaten

320g sheet reduced-fat puff pastry (270g used)

200g Tenderstem broccoli

200g mangetout

1   Toss the steak and flour together in a large bowl and season to taste. Mist a large, lidded, nonstick pan with cooking spray, put over a medium heat and cook the beef for 5 minutes until brown all over. You may need to do this in batches. Transfer the beef to a plate.

2   Mist the pan with more cooking spray. Add the onion, carrots and mushrooms and cook for 7-8 minutes until soft, then return the beef to the pan with its juices and add the ale, stock, bay leaf and herbs. Cover and simmer for 2 hours until the meat is tender.

3   Put the cornflour in a small bowl with 2 tablespoons of the liquid from the pan. Whisk in the Marmite, then stir into the pan with the beef. Cook, uncovered, for 15 minutes until the sauce has reduced and thickened. Remove and discard the bay leaf and herbs.

4   Preheat the oven to 200°C, fan 180°C, gas mark 6. Transfer the stew to a 1.5-litre baking dish. Brush the edges of the dish with the egg and cover with the pastry, pressing it to the sides of the dish and crimping the edges with a fork. Trim off and discard the excess, then cut three slits in the top of the pastry using a sharp knife. Brush the egg all over. Bake for 25-30 minutes until the pastry is golden.

5   Meanwhile, cook the broccoli and mangetout in a steamer for 5 minutes until just tender, then serve with the pie.

The pie filling can be frozen in an airtight container for up to 2 months.

Cook's tip
Try serving this with the Bean & caramelised shallot mash, p202, between 6 for an extra 1 SmartPoint per serving.

 10   **SmartPoints value per serving**

Chicken katsu curry

serves 4   prep time 20 minutes   cook time 20 minutes

In this easy version of the popular Japanese dish, the chicken is browned in a pan, then baked, instead of deep fried. The sauce is mildly spiced.

50g plain flour

75g panko breadcrumbs

2 large eggs, lightly beaten

4 x 165g skinless chicken breast fillets

Calorie controlled cooking spray

70g wild rocket

100g sushi ginger

FOR THE KATSU SAUCE

Calorie controlled cooking spray

1 onion, roughly chopped

2cm piece fresh ginger, peeled and grated

1 large garlic clove, crushed

1 tablespoon medium curry powder

1 tablespoon plain flour

400ml chicken stock, made with 1 stock cube

½ tablespoon light soy sauce

2 teaspoons clear honey

1 Line a baking tray with baking paper and place a wire rack on top. Preheat the oven to 200°C, fan 180°C, gas mark 6.

2 Put the flour, breadcrumbs and eggs into 3 shallow bowls. Put the chicken fillets between two pieces of nonstick baking paper and bash with a rolling pin until the chicken is about 1cm thick.

3 Dip each of the chicken fillets in the flour, then the egg and finally the breadcrumbs. Mist a large frying pan with cooking spray and put over a medium heat. Once hot, add the chicken and cook for 1 minute each side until golden, then transfer to the wire rack on the baking tray and cook in the oven for 10 minutes.

4 While the chicken is cooking, make the sauce. Mist a large nonstick pan with cooking spray and put over a medium heat. Add the onion and cook for 6-8 minutes until softened, then add the ginger and garlic and cook for 1 minute. Add the curry powder and flour and cook for a further 1 minute.

5 Gradually stir in the stock, then add the soy sauce and honey, stirring to combine. Bring to a boil, then reduce the heat and simmer for 10 minutes, until thickened. Allow the sauce to cool slightly, then transfer to a blender and blitz until smooth. Season to taste.

6 Toss the rocket with the sushi ginger. Slice the chicken and serve with the sauce drizzled over, with the salad on the side.

Cook's tip

Serve this with the Spiced cauliflower 'rice', p201, for no extra SmartPoints per serving.

 5 SmartPoints value per serving

Turkey & chilli meatballs

serves 4   freezable   prep time 10 minutes + chilling   cook time 15 minutes

Upgrade your usual spaghetti and meatballs with this version made with turkey mince – they're just as tasty, and make the perfect partner to wholewheat tagliatelle.

500g turkey breast mince

75g fresh wholemeal breadcrumbs

1 egg, lightly beaten

½ onion, finely chopped

2 garlic cloves, crushed

½ teaspoon chilli flakes

Grated zest of ½ lemon

Calorie controlled cooking spray

400g cherry tomatoes, 200g halved and 200g left whole

350g wholewheat tagliatelle

Small handful fresh basil, roughly torn

2 tablespoons grated Parmesan, to serve

1   In a large bowl, combine the mince, breadcrumbs, egg, onion, garlic, chilli flakes and lemon zest. Season to taste, then form into 24 meatballs using your hands. Place the meatballs on a baking tray lined with baking paper, then chill for 1 hour.

2   Mist a large, lidded, nonstick frying pan with cooking spray and set over a low heat. Add the meatballs and cook for 5 minutes, turning halfway through, until just golden. Add all of the tomatoes to the pan along with 100ml water, then cover and cook for 8-10 minutes, stirring occasionally, until the meatballs are cooked through and the tomatoes have started to break down. Remove the lid, increase the heat to high and simmer the meatballs and sauce for a further 5 minutes.

3   Meanwhile, cook the tagliatelle to pack instructions. Drain, then add the pasta to the meatballs and sauce and gently stir to combine. Stir through half of the basil, then serve with the remaining basil and the Parmesan sprinkled over the top.

The meatballs can be frozen in an airtight container for up to 2 months.

10   **SmartPoints value per serving**

Family favourite
'On the table in less than 30 minutes are magic words in my house. That's why this dish has become one of our weekday staples.' **NADINE**

Tomato, pepper & lentil soup

serves 4   **freezable**   **prep time 10 minutes**   **cook time 30 minutes**

Packed with flavour and colour, this delicious soup is a great one to make ahead and freeze. Without the roll, it's only 1 SmartPoint per serving.

½ tablespoon olive oil

1 onion, finely chopped

2 red peppers, deseeded and roughly chopped

2 garlic cloves, crushed

500g tomatoes, roughly chopped

400g tin chopped tomatoes

80g red lentils

2 teaspoons dried oregano

1 litre hot vegetable stock, made with 2 stock cubes

4 x 65g crusty brown bread rolls, to serve

1   Heat the oil in a large pan over a medium heat, add the onion and peppers and cook for 6-8 minutes until soft. Add the garlic and fresh tomatoes and cook for another 5 minutes.

2   Add the chopped tomatoes, red lentils, 1 teaspoon of the oregano and the vegetable stock and cook for 30 minutes until the vegetables and lentils are tender.

3   Season to taste, then transfer the soup to a blender (or use a stick blender) and blitz until smooth. Serve with the remaining oregano sprinkled over and the crusty bread rolls on the side.

The soup can be frozen in an airtight container for up to 3 months.

6   **SmartPoints value per serving**

Cook's tip
Add spice to your soup with 1½ tablespoons harissa paste. The SmartPoints will remain the same.

Easy roast chicken dinner

serves 4   **prep time 15 minutes**   **cook time 40 minutes**

This speedy version of a traditional roast dinner includes lots of delicious veg, and makes an ideal mid-week winter meal.

800g new potatoes

5 garlic cloves, unpeeled

2 large carrots, cut into small chunks

1 large red onion, cut into wedges

1 tablespoon roughly chopped fresh rosemary

3 sprigs fresh thyme, leaves picked and roughly chopped, plus extra sprigs, to serve

1 tablespoon olive oil

1 teaspoon dried mixed herbs

4 x 165g skinless chicken breast fillets

400g Tenderstem broccoli

4 small shallots, peeled and quartered

400g frozen peas

300ml hot chicken stock, made with ½ stock cube

Freshly ground black pepper, to serve

1 Preheat the oven to 200°C, fan 180°C, gas mark 6. Put the potatoes, garlic, carrots, onion and fresh herbs in a roasting tin, then add the oil and toss to coat. Season to taste and roast for 20 minutes.

2 Sprinkle the dried mixed herbs over the chicken breasts. Nestle the chicken among the vegetables and add the broccoli. Cook the mixture for another 20 minutes, stirring the vegetables once.

3 Meanwhile, put the shallots and peas in a small pan with the chicken stock and simmer over a medium heat for 7 minutes. Serve the peas with the chicken and vegetables, spooning over any extra liquid from the peas and sprinkling over the black pepper before serving.

5 **SmartPoints value per serving**

Sunday lunch
'Love roast dinners? Love an easy life? This recipe is made specially for you. It's one of my favourites.' **JONNY**

Melt-in-the-middle fishcakes

serves 4 **freezable** **prep time 20 minutes** **cook time 45 minutes**

With a crispy crumb coating and melting cheesy centre, these easy fishcakes served with butternut squash chips are irresistible.

500g potatoes, cut into chunks

1 butternut squash, peeled, deseeded and cut into 1cm-thick chips

Calorie controlled cooking spray

80g frozen peas, defrosted

200g cooked salmon, flaked

½ tablespoon snipped fresh chives

40g half-fat Cheddar cheese

30g plain flour

1 egg, lightly beaten

50g panko breadcrumbs

Green salad, to serve

1 Put the potatoes in a large pan of boiling water and cook for 15-20 minutes until tender, then drain and mash. Set aside.

2 Preheat the oven to 200°C, fan 180°C, gas mark 6. Spread the butternut squash chips out on a large baking tray, mist with cooking spray and bake for 30-35 minutes, turning halfway, until cooked through.

3 Meanwhile, add the peas, salmon and chives to the mash and season to taste. Stir to combine, then form the salmon and mash mixture into 4 patties. Cut the cheese into 4 pieces and push 1 into the middle of each fishcake, ensuring it's enclosed in the mixture. Put the flour, egg and breadcrumbs into three separate bowls. Dip each fishcake in the flour, then the egg and finally the breadcrumbs, ensuring they're fully coated.

4 Mist a large, nonstick, ovenproof frying pan with cooking spray and fry the fishcakes for 2 minutes on each side until golden. Transfer the pan to the oven with the chips and cook for 10 minutes until golden and piping hot. Serve with the chips and the salad on the side.

The fishcakes can be frozen in an airtight container for up to 3 months.

Cook's tip
Try serving the fishcakes with the Roasted beetroot, p202, for an extra 1 SmartPoint per serving.

6 **SmartPoints value per serving**

Vegan sausages with carrot & swede mash

serves 4   **prep time 5 minutes**   **cook time 20 minutes**

This vegan version of the classic British favourite includes a mixed vegetable mash, which makes a delicious change from potatoes.

8 Quorn vegan Cumberland sausages
Calorie controlled cooking spray
1kg pack chopped carrot and swede
¼ teaspoon ground nutmeg
1 tablespoon agave syrup
1 tablespoon wholegrain mustard
1 teaspoon white wine vinegar
300ml hot vegetable stock, made with 1 stock cube
2 teaspoons cornflour
2 sprigs fresh thyme, leaves picked and roughly chopped, to serve

1   Preheat the oven to 180°C, fan 160°C, gas mark 4. Put the sausages in a roasting tin, mist with cooking spray and cook for 20 minutes, turning halfway through.

2   Put the carrot and swede in a large pan of boiling water and cook for 20 minutes or until tender, then drain and mash. Season to taste, then stir in the nutmeg.

3   Meanwhile, whisk the agave syrup, mustard, vinegar and stock together in a small pan and put over a medium heat. Bring to a boil, then reduce the heat and simmer for 8-10 minutes until slightly reduced. Put the cornflour in a small bowl and whisk in a little of the stock until well combined. Stir the mixture into the gravy and cook for 2 minutes until thickened.

4   Serve the sausages on the mash with the thyme scattered on top and the gravy poured over.

7   **SmartPoints value per serving**

Classic favourite
'Just because I'm vegan doesn't mean I don't love sausages! I guarantee this dish competes on a level playing field with your regular bangers and mash.' **ELISHA**

Chicken cacciatore

serves 4   **freezable**   **prep time 10 minutes**   **cook time 35 minutes**

Made with onion, garlic and tomato, this take on the classic Italian 'hunter's chicken' is flavourful and warming during colder days.

Calorie controlled cooking spray
4 bacon medallions, roughly chopped
4 x 165g skinless chicken breast fillets
1 onion, chopped
2 garlic cloves, crushed
4 tablespoons balsamic vinegar
400g tin chopped tomatoes
150ml chicken stock, made using 1 stock cube
1 tablespoon tomato purée
Small handful fresh thyme sprigs
Small handful fresh rosemary sprigs
200g pitted black olives in brine, drained

1   Mist a large, lidded, nonstick frying pan with cooking spray and put over a medium-high heat. Add the bacon and cook for 2 minutes, or until golden. Transfer to a plate and set aside.

2   Add the chicken fillets to the pan, season to taste and sear on each side for 3-4 minutes, or until brown all over. Transfer to the plate with the bacon.

3   Add the onion and garlic to the pan, reduce the heat to low and cook for 6-8 minutes until soft, adding a splash of water if the mixture starts to stick. Add the balsamic vinegar and bring to a gentle simmer, then cook until slightly reduced. Add the chopped tomatoes, stock, tomato purée and herbs, then stir to combine.

4   Stir in the bacon, then nestle the chicken fillets into the sauce. Cover and simmer for 15 minutes, or until the chicken is cooked through and the sauce has thickened. Add the olives and simmer for a further 5 minutes, then season to taste and serve.

The cacciatore can be frozen in an airtight container for up to 2 months.

Cook's tip
Serve this with a ZeroPoint green veg such as Tenderstem broccoli and some new potatoes – 150g per person would be an extra 3 SmartPoints per serving.

3   SmartPoints value per serving

Curried parsnip & carrot soup

serves 4   **freezable**   **prep time 15 minutes**   **cook time 50 minutes**

Earthy, sweet parsnips are a classic winter vegetable. In this wonderfully warming soup, they're teamed with carrots and a hint of spice.

Calorie controlled cooking spray

1 onion, finely chopped

2 celery sticks, finely chopped

1 garlic clove, crushed

½ tablespoon curry powder

½ teaspoon ground ginger

300g parsnips, roughly chopped

300g carrots, roughly chopped

1 litre vegetable stock, made with 2 stock cubes

2 tablespoons chopped fresh coriander

Lemon wedges, to serve

Freshly ground black pepper, to serve

1 Mist a large, lidded, nonstick pan with cooking spray, put over a medium heat and fry the onion, celery and garlic for 6-8 minutes until soft. Add the curry powder and ginger and cook, stirring, for another 1 minute.

2 Add the parsnips, carrots and stock. Season to taste and bring to a boil, then reduce the heat and simmer, covered, for 40 minutes.

3 Add half the coriander, then, using a stick blender, blitz until smooth. Serve the soup with the lemon wedges on the side to squeeze over and the remaining coriander and some black pepper scattered over the top.

The soup can be frozen in an airtight container for up to 3 months.

3 **SmartPoints value per serving**

Winter warmer

'Where would we be without soup? I always have a batch of soup in the freezer to use on busy days, and this one's perfect for the colder months.' **SELEN**

Bean & sausage cassoulet

serves 4   **freezable**   **prep time 10 minutes**   **cook time 35 minutes**

A hearty, French-inspired stew that's packed with rich flavour. This recipe freezes well, so it's a great dish to batch cook and save for later.

Calorie controlled cooking spray

8 reduced-fat pork sausages

1 onion, thinly sliced

1 stick celery, diced

1 carrot, diced

3 garlic cloves, thinly sliced

1 tablespoon tomato purée

1 teaspoon smoked paprika

400g tin chopped tomatoes

400g tin cannellini beans, drained and rinsed

250ml beef stock, made with 1 stock cube

Small handful fresh thyme, leaves picked

2 bay leaves

Large handful fresh flat-leaf parsley, roughly chopped

1   Mist a large, deep, lidded, nonstick pan with cooking spray and put over a medium-high heat. Add the sausages and cook for 6-8 minutes, turning occasionally, until golden brown all over. Transfer to a plate.

2   Add the onion, celery, carrot and garlic to the pan and cook for 6-8 minutes until softened. Add the tomato purée and paprika and cook for a further 1 minute.

3   Add the tomatoes, cannellini beans, beef stock, thyme leaves and bay leaves. Season to taste and stir to combine, then return the sausages to the pan. Cover and simmer over a low heat for 15 minutes, until the sausages are cooked through and the sauce has reduced slightly.

4   Remove and discard the bay leaves, then serve the cassoulet with the parsley scattered over the top.

The cassoulet can be frozen in an airtight container for up to 2 months.

4   **SmartPoints value per serving**

Cook's tip
Try serving this with the Chilli-roasted Brussels sprouts, p201, for an extra 1 SmartPoint per serving.

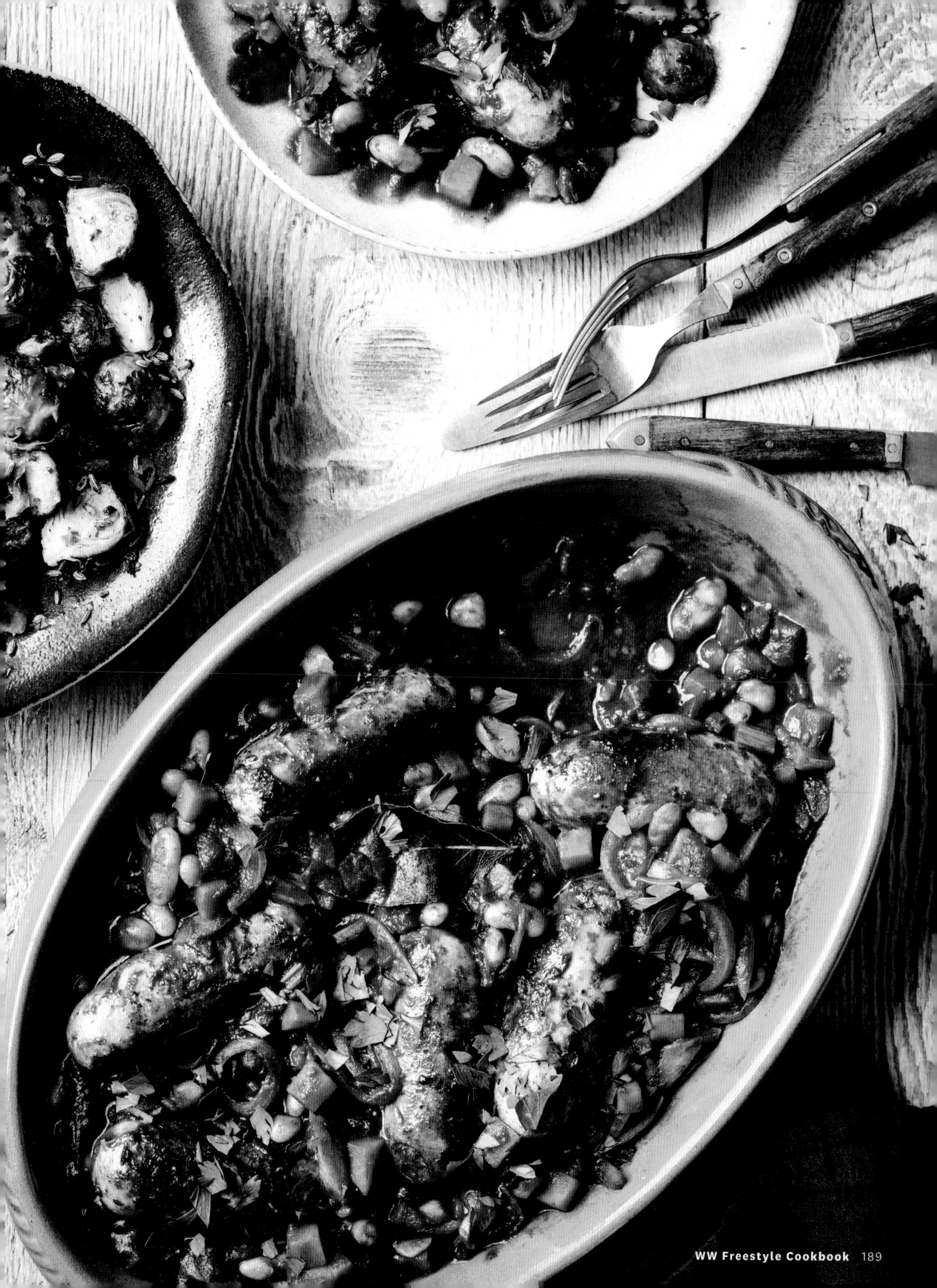

Salmon fish fingers

serves 4   **prep time 20 minutes**   **cook time 10 minutes**

Ready-made fish fingers never tasted this good! You can use almost any kind of fish you like, but we've used salmon in this recipe for maximum flavour.

100g stale wholemeal bread

2 tablespoons grated Parmesan

1 tablespoon dried mixed herbs

2 tablespoons olive oil

1 large egg, beaten

50g plain flour

4 x 120g skinless salmon fillets

300g frozen peas

1 tablespoon lemon juice

1 tablespoon fresh mint, finely chopped

2 tablespoons 0% fat natural Greek yogurt

Lemon wedges, to serve

1 Preheat the oven to 220°C, fan 200°C, gas mark 7. Put the bread in a food processor and blitz to fine crumbs. Tip into a medium bowl, stir in the Parmesan and mixed herbs, and season to taste. Drizzle over the oil and stir to combine. Put the beaten egg and plain flour in two separate shallow bowls.

2 Cut each salmon fillet into 4 chunky fish fingers. Working in batches, dip the fish fingers in the flour, then the beaten egg and finally the breadcrumbs. Arrange the breaded fish fingers on a large baking tray lined with baking paper and bake for 8-10 minutes, turning halfway through, until golden and crisp.

3 Meanwhile, cook the peas in boiling water for 3 minutes. Drain, then return to the pan and add the lemon juice, mint and yogurt. Season to taste, then lightly mash using a potato masher. Serve the salmon fish fingers with the crushed peas on the side and the lemon wedges to squeeze over.

6   SmartPoints value per serving

Cook's tip
Try serving this with the Roasted fennel, chickpeas & potatoes, p202, for an extra 3 SmartPoints per serving.

Pork rendang

serves 4   **prep time 10 minutes**   **cook time 2 hours 45 minutes**

This spicy stew originated in Indonesia and features a blend of warming, fragrant spices. The pork is slow-cooked until it's falling apart, making it tender and flavoursome.

Calorie controlled cooking spray

2 onions, finely chopped

2 tablespoon rendang curry paste

2 garlic cloves, crushed

3cm piece fresh ginger, peeled and grated

1 red chilli, deseeded and finely chopped, plus extra sliced chilli, to serve

800g lean pork shoulder, diced

500ml chicken stock, made with 1 stock cube

150ml reduced-fat coconut milk

Small handful fresh coriander, stalks and leaves finely chopped, plus extra sprigs to serve

600g cauliflower rice

Lime slices, to serve

1 Mist a large, lidded, nonstick casserole dish with cooking spray and fry the onions for 6-8 minutes until soft. Add the curry paste, garlic, ginger and chilli and fry for another 2 minutes.

2 Add the pork and stir-fry for 3-4 minutes until just browned. Add the stock, coconut milk and coriander, and stir to combine. Cover, reduce the heat and gently simmer for 2 hours 15 minutes, stirring occasionally.

3 Using a slotted spoon, transfer the pork to a plate, then increase the heat. Gently simmer the sauce for 15 minutes until reduced. Meanwhile, shred the pork using two forks, then stir through the sauce.

4 Put the cauliflower 'rice' in a microwave-safe bowl, then cover and cook on high for 4 minutes, stirring halfway through. Serve the curry and cauliflower 'rice' in bowls with the extra chilli slices and coriander scattered on top and the lime slices on the side to squeeze over.

8 SmartPoints value per serving

Cook's tip
To make the cauliflower 'rice', put 600g cauliflower florets in a food processor and pulse briefly until it's the texture of rice.

Slow-cooked salmon with chickpeas

serves 4   **prep time 10 minutes**   **cook time 40 minutes**

Sharp lemon and sweet honey help to lift this filling dish, which combines ZeroPoint salmon, chickpeas and young leaf spinach.

2 x 400g tins chickpeas, drained and rinsed

Grated zest and juice of 1 lemon

Calorie controlled cooking spray

2 garlic cloves, crushed

300g young leaf spinach

4 x 120g skinless salmon fillets

2 tablespoons olive oil

1 small shallot, very finely chopped

1 teaspoon Dijon mustard

1 teaspoon clear honey

1 tablespoon chopped fresh dill, to serve

1   Preheat the oven to 120°C, fan 100°C, gas mark ½. Put the chickpeas in a large bowl and roughly mash. Season to taste, then add the lemon zest and toss to combine. Transfer to a 20cm x 20cm baking dish.

2   Mist a large nonstick pan with cooking spray and put over a medium-high heat. Add the garlic and cook for 1 minute or until fragrant, then add the spinach and cook for a further 4-5 minutes, until the spinach has wilted. Season to taste, then add to the dish with the chickpeas.

3   Arrange the salmon fillets over the spinach and chickpea mixture and season to taste. Drizzle with 1 tablespoon of the olive oil, then bake for 35 minutes, or until the salmon is just cooked through.

4   Meanwhile, make the dressing. Put the shallot, lemon juice, mustard and honey in a small bowl and season to taste. Gradually whisk in the remaining olive oil. To serve, drizzle the vinaigrette over the salmon, then scatter over the fresh dill.

3   **SmartPoints value per serving**

Cook's tip
Try serving this with the Wild rice & lentil salad, p201, for an extra 4 SmartPoints per serving.

Blue cheese cannelloni

serves 4   freezable   prep time 20 minutes   cook time 1 hour 5 minutes

We think of this as an Italian dish, but it's also popular in Spain, where it's traditionally eaten on Boxing Day. This recipe features a classic soft cheese and spinach filling.

Calorie controlled cooking spray
250g chestnut mushrooms, quartered
2 x 400g tins chopped tomatoes
1½ teaspoons dried oregano
1 tablespoon finely chopped basil
2 teaspoons red wine vinegar
300g young spinach
200g low-fat soft cheese
60g grated vegetarian Italian-style hard cheese, 15g reserved
50g Stilton, crumbled
2 egg yolks
¼ teaspoon ground nutmeg
180g dried cannelloni pasta tubes
Green leaf salad, to serve

1   Mist a large nonstick pan with cooking spray and put over a medium heat. Add the mushrooms and cook for 5-6 minutes until tender, then add the tomatoes, oregano, basil and vinegar, reduce the heat and gently simmer for 20 minutes.

2   Preheat the oven to 200°C, fan 180°C, gas mark 6. Put the spinach in a colander and pour over a full kettle of boiling water until the spinach wilts. Press out as much water as you can using the back of a spoon, then roughly chop the spinach. In a large bowl, combine the spinach, cheeses, egg yolks and nutmeg. Season to taste and stir to combine.

3   Fill a piping bag with the cheese mixture and pipe into the cannelloni tubes until they're about half full. Pour a little of the sauce into the dish, then put the filled tubes on top and pour over the remaining sauce. Sprinkle over the reserved grated hard cheese. Cover the dish tightly with kitchen foil and bake for 20 minutes, then uncover and bake for a further 20 minutes. Serve with the salad on the side.

You can freeze the unbaked cannelloni in the baking dish, wrapped in foil, for up to 1 month. Defrost before continuing to cook as in the recipe.

10   SmartPoints value per serving

Perfect match

'Blue cheese and spinach are a great flavour pairing. And you can use frozen spinach in place of fresh – just be sure to squeeze out any excess water before adding in step 2.' **ELLA**

Bacon & cabbage braise with chicken

serves 4   **prep time 5 minutes**   **cook time 25 minutes**

Cabbage is often overlooked, but it's the star of the show in this hearty take on the traditional Irish dish of bacon and cabbage.

Calorie controlled cooking spray

4 x 165g skinless chicken breast fillets

1 onion, finely chopped

1 garlic clove, crushed

8 smoked bacon medallions, cut into 3cm strips

1 small Savoy cabbage, trimmed and thickly shredded

400g tin cannellini beans, drained and rinsed

400ml hot chicken stock, made with 1 stock cube

4 x 65g crusty white bread rolls, to serve

1   Preheat the oven to 200°C, fan 180°C, gas mark 6. Mist a large, lidded, nonstick pan with cooking spray and brown the chicken for 2-3 minutes on each side. Transfer to a roasting tin and roast for 25 minutes.

2   Meanwhile, add the onion to the pan and cook for 6-8 minutes until soft, then add the garlic and bacon and cook, stirring, for 4-5 minutes until the bacon begins to crisp at the edges. Stir in the cabbage and allow to wilt for 2 minutes, then stir in the beans and chicken stock. Cover and simmer for 10-12 minutes until the beans have heated through and the stock has reduced slightly.

3   Season to taste, then serve the stew topped with the chicken and the bread rolls on the side.

6   **SmartPoints value per serving**

Cook's tip
Shred the chicken into the stew if you prefer. Without the rolls, the dish is only 1 SmartPoint per serving.

Winter sides

Fancy a little more? These delicious side ideas will bulk up your meals and help warm you up.

Wild rice & lentil salad

serves 4   prep time 10 minutes   cook time 2 minutes

Cook a 250g pouch microwave **long grain brown and wild rice** to pack instructions. Put in a large bowl, season to taste, then add a 400g tin drained and rinsed **green lentils**, 2 tablespoons roughly chopped **pistachio nuts**, 2 tablespoons finely chopped **fresh dill**, 1 tablespoon each finely chopped **fresh mint** and **fresh coriander**, 1 tablespoon roughly chopped **dried cranberries**, the grated zest of ½ **lemon**, ½ thinly sliced **red onion** and 1 teaspoon **ground cumin**. Stir to combine, then serve.

4 SmartPoints value per serving

Spiced cauliflower 'rice'

serves 4   prep time 5 minutes   cook time 6 minutes

Cut 1 trimmed **cauliflower** into florets, then put in a food processor. Blitz until roughly the texture of rice, then transfer to a microwave-safe bowl. Cover with a plate, leaving a small gap, then cook on high for 5-6 minutes. Stir through ¼ teaspoon each of **garlic granules**, **ground cumin** and **ground coriander**, ½ teaspoon **mild chilli powder** and 2 tablespoons chopped **fresh coriander**. Season to taste, then sprinkle over a little extra **mild chilli powder** to serve.

0 SmartPoints value per serving

Chilli-roasted Brussels sprouts

serves 4   prep time 10 minutes   cook time 25 minutes

Preheat the oven to 190°C, fan 170°C, gas mark 5. Trim and halve 800g **Brussels sprouts**, then toss together in a roasting tin with 1 tablespoon **olive oil** and ½ tablespoon each of **chilli flakes** and **fennel seeds**. Season to taste, then roast for 20-25 minutes until tender, tossing once halfway through. Serve with 1 deseeded and thinly sliced **red chilli** scattered over.

1 SmartPoints value per serving

Winter sides

Bean & caramelised shallot mash
serves 4   prep time 10 minutes   cook time 30 minutes

Heat ½ tablespoon **olive oil** in a large pan over a medium-low heat. Add 4 large thinly sliced **shallots** and cook, stirring, for 15-20 minutes. Add 3 crushed **garlic cloves** and cook for another 2 minutes, then add 2 x 400g tins drained and rinsed **cannellini beans** and 2 x 400g tins drained and rinsed **butter beans**, along with 400ml hot vegetable stock made with 1 **stock cube**. Increase the heat, then simmer until reduced by three quarters. Season to taste, then add ½ tablespoon picked and chopped **fresh rosemary leaves**. Using a stick blender (or a handheld potato masher), blitz to a purée. Stir in 4 tablespoons **fat-free natural yogurt** and the juice of ½ **lemon**, then serve with extra picked and chopped **fresh rosemary leaves** scattered over.

 1 SmartPoints value per serving

Roasted beetroot
serves 4   prep time 10 minutes   cook time 1 hour

Preheat the oven to 200°C, fan 180°C, gas mark 6. Trim and peel 1kg **beetroot** and cut into 3cm wedges. Put in a large roasting tin with ½ tablespoon **olive oil**, 1 tablespoon **balsamic vinegar** and 5 unpeeled **garlic cloves**. Toss to combine and season to taste. Roast for 1 hour, or until sticky and tender. Serve with **lemon wedges** to squeeze over.

1 SmartPoints value per serving

Roasted fennel, chickpeas & potatoes
serves 4   prep time 10 minutes   cook time 45 minutes

Preheat the oven to 200°C, fan 180°C, gas mark 6. Trim 3 large **fennel bulbs** and cut into wedges, reserving the fronds. Put the fennel in a roasting tin with 2 crushed **garlic cloves**, the juice of ½ **lemon**, ½ tablespoon **olive oil**, 400g sliced **new potatoes** and ½ tablespoon **fennel seeds**, then season and toss to combine. Cover the tin with kitchen foil and bake for 30 minutes. Remove the foil, stir the veg and increase the heat to 220°C, fan 200°C, gas mark 7. Cook for 10 minutes, then add a 400g tin drained and rinsed **chickpeas** and cook for another 5 minutes. Stir in 2 tablespoons chopped **fresh dill** and the fennel fronds, then serve with **lemon slices**.

3 SmartPoints value per serving

Winter snacks & desserts

As nights draw in and days grow colder, who doesn't love tucking into a pud or a comforting snack? We've got just the thing...

Gingerbread people
makes 25
prep time 15 minutes + chilling
cook time 20 minutes

Put 75g **light brown soft sugar**, 1½ tablespoons **golden syrup** and 1 tablespoon **black treacle** in a small pan set over a low heat and cook, stirring, until the sugar has dissolved. Stir in 95g **low-fat spread** until melted, then remove from the heat and, using a wooden spoon, stir in 230g **plain flour**, 2 teaspoons **ground ginger** and 1 teaspoon **ground cinnamon** until a soft dough forms. Using your hands, form the dough into a disc and wrap in clingfilm, then chill for 30 minutes. Preheat the oven to 180°C, fan 160°C, gas mark 4. Dust the work surface with **plain flour** and roll the dough out to a 3mm thickness. Using a 7cm gingerbread man cutter, cut out 25 biscuits, rerolling the trimmings as needed. Transfer to a baking sheet lined with baking paper, then bake for 15 minutes. Transfer to a wire rack to cool. To decorate the biscuits combine 30g **icing sugar** and enough water to make a thin icing, start with 1 teaspoon, then pipe over. The biscuits will keep in an airtight container for up to 5 days.

 3 **SmartPoints value per biscuit**

Cook's tip
Use other shaped cutters, such as stars, trees or snowflakes, to make these even more festive.

'The whole
house smells
like Christmas
when these are
in the oven.'
ELLA

Crunchy chilli lentils

serves 4
prep time 5 minutes
cook time 30 minutes

Preheat the oven to 200°C, fan 180°C, gas mark 6. Put 2 x 400g tins drained and rinsed **green lentils**, 1 tablespoon **vegetable oil**, 1½ teaspoons **chilli flakes** and 1 teaspoon **garlic salt** in a large bowl and toss to combine. Spread the lentils out on a large baking tray in a single layer, then bake for 12 minutes. Stir and bake for another 12-15 minutes, until crunchy. Season to taste. Once cool, store in an airtight container for up to 2 days.

1 SmartPoints value per serving

Clementine filo mince pies

makes 12
prep time 15 minutes
cook time 15 minutes

Preheat the oven to 200°C, fan 180°C, gas mark 6. Mist a 12-hole nonstick muffin tin with **calorie controlled cooking spray**. Lay 1 sheet **ready-rolled filo pastry** (you'll need 220g pastry in total) on the work surface and mist with additional **cooking spray**. Cut the pastry into 6 rectangles. Layer 1 pastry rectangle over a second on the diagonal, then gently press into one hole of the muffin tin; repeat with the remaining rectangles. Repeat with the 3 additional sheets of filo pastry to fill the tin. In a medium bowl, combine the zest and chopped flesh of 1 **clementine** and 100g **mincemeat**. Spoon the filling over the pastry, then fold at the top to enclose. Bake for 12-15 minutes, until golden and bubbling. Let cool in the tin for 2 minutes, then transfer to a wire rack to cool completely. Sprinkle over 1 teaspoon **icing sugar** to serve.

3 SmartPoints value per mince pie

Flourless chocolate puddings

makes 4
prep time 5 minutes
cook time 20 minutes

Preheat the oven to 180°C, fan 160°C, gas mark 4. Put 50g **ground almonds**, 4 tablespoons **cocoa powder**, 2 very ripe **bananas** and 2 **eggs** in a food processor and blitz until smooth. Divide between 4 x 200ml ramekins and put on a baking tray. Mix ½ tablespoon **cocoa powder** with 1 tablespoon **light brown soft sugar** and sprinkle over the puddings, then pour 25ml boiling water over the top of each. Bake for 20 minutes, until the sponge springs back when lightly pressed. Spoon 1 tablespoon **fat-free natural yogurt** onto each pudding, then sprinkle over 1 teaspoon **cocoa powder** among the 4 puds to serve.

4 SmartPoints value per pudding

Lemon, ginger & pear mug cakes

makes 6
prep time 15 minutes
cook time 10 minutes

Mist the inside of 6 small mugs or teacups with **calorie controlled cooking spray**. Put 90g **low-fat spread**, 30g **0% fat natural Greek yogurt**, 100g **self-raising flour**, 40g **golden caster sugar**, 1 large **egg** and 1 teaspoon **ground ginger** in a food processor and blitz until smooth. Add 1 ball finely chopped **stem ginger** and the zest of 1 **lemon** and blitz to combine. Put ½ teaspoon **stem ginger syrup** in the base of each mug. Peel, core and roughly chop 3 **pears**, then divide between the mugs, reserving some to serve. Spoon over the cake mixture. Cut 6 small circles from a sheet of baking paper, mist with cooking spray and place over the top of the mugs. Cook 3 cakes at a time in the microwave on high for 5 minutes. Discard the papers and set aside to cool, then serve each cake with the reserved pears and extra **lemon zest** scattered over and with 1 tablespoon **0% fat natural Greek yogurt** spooned over the top.

6 SmartPoints value per mug cake

Meal plans

Breakfast   **Lunch**   **Snack**

Quick & easy

serves 4   **22** **SmartPoints value**

On busy weekdays, you want meals that are simple and speedy, but still tasty and satisfying. Look for all-in-one recipes that are quick to prepare and cook, or ones that don't require cooking.

Breakfast – ready in 10 minutes
Coconut chia porridge p166

 7   **SmartPoints value per serving**

Lunch – ready in 30 minutes
Chinese vegetable stir-fry p46

6   **SmartPoints value per serving**

Dinner – ready in 30 minutes
Bacon & cabbage braise with chicken p198

6   **SmartPoints value per serving**

Snack – ready in 10 minutes
Houmous with crudités p68

 3   **SmartPoints value per serving**

Dinner

Breakfast   **Lunch**   **Dessert**

Family favourites

serves 4   **23**   **SmartPoints value per serving**

Instead of cooking separate meals for other members of the family, choose recipes that will keep everyone happy. Add extras like bread rolls for anyone who's not following WW.

Breakfast
Pancakes with bacon & bananas p76

 6   **SmartPoints value per serving**

Lunch
Salmon fish fingers p190

6   **SmartPoints value per serving**

Dinner
Chicken casserole with dumplings p138

 8   **SmartPoints value per serving**

Dessert
Banana & peanut butter 'ice cream' p114

 3   **SmartPoints value per serving**

Dinner

Breakfast Lunch Snack

Lazy weekend

serves 4   20 SmartPoints value

Weekends are the perfect chance to spend a bit more time in the kitchen making recipes that you just can't manage during the week. Think slow-cooked curries and cooked breakfasts.

Breakfast
Veggie fry-up p168

 7 SmartPoints value per serving

Lunch
Greek chicken souvlaki wrap p98

 4 SmartPoints value per serving

Roasted tomato & rocket salad p109

 1 SmartPoints value per serving

Dinner
Aubergine & tomato curry p128

 1 SmartPoints value per serving

Spicy turmeric rice p154

6 SmartPoints value per serving

Snack
Carrot cake snack bites p68

 1 SmartPoints value per bite

Dinner

Breakfast   Lunch   Dessert

Vegetarian

serves 4   **22**   **SmartPoints value**

Even if you're not a full-time veggie, you might want to have the odd meat-free day. With veg, fruit, eggs and fat-free yogurt on the ZeroPoint food list, you're never short of tasty options.

Breakfast
Tropical fruit salad with oats & yogurt p74

 3   **SmartPoints value per serving**

Lunch
Pea & potato fritters with poached eggs p52

 4   **SmartPoints value per serving**

Dinner
Primavera risotto p32

 12   **SmartPoints value per serving**

Dessert
Cinnamon crepes with griddled bananas p66

 3   **SmartPoints value per serving**

Dinner

Breakfast   Lunch   Dessert

Make ahead

serves 4   **21**   SmartPoints value

Keep kitchen time to a minimum on busy days by prepping food in advance. Most soups and pasta sauces are freezable, so all you have to do is heat and eat.

Breakfast
Bircher muesli with peaches p76

 6   SmartPoints value per serving

Lunch
Curried parsnip & carrot soup p186

 3   SmartPoints value per serving

Dinner
Turkey & chilli meatballs p174

 10   SmartPoints value per serving

Dessert
Mango, lime & yogurt ice lollies p68

 2   SmartPoints value per lolly

Breakfast **Lunch** **Dessert**

Gluten free

serves 4   (22)   SmartPoints value

Going gluten free can be a challenge, but when you're cooking from scratch, things get a lot easier. Choose recipes that include seeds and whole grains like quinoa, or rice noodles.

Breakfast
Mushroom & tomato omelette p122

 (0)   SmartPoints value per serving

Lunch
Prawn pad Thai p100

 (7)   SmartPoints value per serving

Dinner
Courgette & turkey lasagne p34

 (8)   SmartPoints value per serving

Dessert
Strawberry sundaes p114

 (7)   SmartPoints value per serving

Dinner

Recipe index

Recipe index